D0069934

*Internet
Research*

Internet Research

Theory and Practice

SECOND EDITION

by
NED L. FIELDEN

McFarland & Company, Inc., Publishers
Jefferson, North Carolina, and London

Library of Congress Cataloguing-in-Publication Data

Fielden, Ned L., 1954–
    Internet research : theory and practice / by Ned L. Fielden — 2nd ed.
        p.   cm.
    Includes bibliographical references and index.
    ISBN 0-7864-1099-X (softcover : 50# alkaline paper) ∞
    1. Computer network resources.   2. Electronic information
resource searching.   I. Title.
    ZA4201.F54   2001
    025.04 — dc21   00-54807

British Library cataloguing data are available

©2001 Ned L. Fielden. All rights reserved

*No part of this book may be reproduced or transmitted in any form
or by any means, electronic or mechanical, including photocopying
or recording, or by any information storage and retrieval system,
without permission in writing from the publisher.*

Cover image © 2000 Index Stock.

Manufactured in the United States of America

McFarland & Company, Inc., Publishers
    Box 611, Jefferson, North Carolina 28640
    www.mcfarlandpub.com

To Gene, Maggie and Lucy

Acknowledgments

No book is an island. I have benefited from a great many colleagues, friends and family members in the making of this second edition. Librarians around the country have demonstrated their traditional cheerful willingness to share and help with information on all sorts of topics. In particular, I want to thank my colleagues at San Francisco State University: Darlene Tong, Linda Bowles-Adarkwa, Stuart Hall, LaVonne Jacobsen, Jeff Rosen, Chris Mays, Caroline Harnly, Ann Kennedy, Mitch Turitz and Gina Castro for their work, often in the realm of subject resources on the Internet. Also, thanks go to colleagues at Sonoma State University: Barbara Butler, Paula Hammett and Raye Lynn Thomas. The friendly pragmatic members of the discussion group NETTRAIN under the lead of Diane Kovacs have proved enduringly helpful on a range of issues, and there are many more librarians, faculty and grad students around the world whose Internet work I have examined and who have directly or indirectly provided helpful information.

My family astonishes me with the level of support they offer. My parents Lee and Connie Fielden are perennial optimists—"how is it going?" they will ask. My 3-year old Aaron knows only that sometimes I am "working on the computer." Teenagers Maggie and Gene put up with distracted looks, a steady view of the back of my head while I am hunched over the keyboard at home, and general emotional havoc. My spouse Lucy, bless her soul, puts up with foul moods, habitual cussings at software or the printer, and unreasonable and systemic neglect while I am in the throes of writing.

To all, many thanks for your help, indulgence, cheerful advice, and goodwill.

Ned Fielden
Berkeley, September 2000

Contents

Preface to the Second Edition

When this book was first conceived, there were relatively few good texts that productively discussed academic research utilizing Internet protocols and finding tools. Since then, a number of works have come out and the field is now crowded with a multitude of specialist books—niches that are often filled quite competently. Also since this book first appeared, developments in World Wide Web search engines and the way the Web has evolved meant that there are more issues to discuss and update.

This work has one primary audience—college and university students who envision utilizing the Internet for their studies. My courses at San Francisco State University cover database searching, research methods, and developed mastery of journal indexes and Internet locating tools, and this work was originally conceived as support to this end. Faculty, other librarians, and other instructors engaged in Internet training may find this book helpful either as a text or as a supplement to their own activities. I hope this book has some appeal to a more general educated audience, but in all cases, the emphasis is on academic use of the Internet for research. I do not think that the process of research at the college level is easy to understand, and I believe that everyone engaged in research can improve their methods and results.

A second edition must promise more than the first, and I hope this is true for this second effort. Updates occur throughout the book, particularly in the subject areas of chapter five and the bibliography. Several areas have been expanded as well, with discussions about a number of features that the search engines provide, the scholar's workstation model of research, the effects of how Web documents are constructed on their "findability" in search engines, and a number of smaller topics. The text has been revised throughout, with improved descriptions, screen capture photos and new material where appropriate.

Obviously updating means including Internet addresses. URLs have an unfortunate tendency to go dead or move elsewhere, which means that a proper update of addresses is always necessary for any book devoted to Internet resources. While in the first edition I made an attempt to use only "stable" addresses, Web time is a rapidly evolving soup of change.

To address this last situation, I have made a list of all the links supplied in the book to post on my personal university homepage, which I will update regularly for the life of the second edition — at least until 2004 — at http://userwww.sfsu.edu/~fielden/internetresearch.htm. As a bonus, additional Internet addresses of interest will be added (as discovered) so that the online set of links will be richer than the list compiled for the book.

Like it or not, the Internet is maturing, but the process (as in humans) is not always pleasant. Unintended consequences dominate. Who would ever have thought that the raging commercial pressures of the Web would pollute the process of search engine site location? Okay, a lot of people did, but still — what a mess. At every conference I have attended with search engine designers present, the number one problem mentioned is spam. How to get rid of the junk. This is a common problem for everyone who uses the Internet to find information, and one that will probably be vexing forever.

It is also an ancient issue, of course. When writing (and discursive and reflective thinking) was done by fewer people (when intellectuals were a small percentage of the population) and the output of information was smaller, it was much easier to utilize only quality information. Now that everyone and his brother can put up a Webpage on any topic in the world, post it to the Net or broadcast it internationally, the researcher is in a much more complicated position. Sifting through acres of data to end up with a tiny little piece of information of dubious quality is not everyone's idea of pleasure.

When you factor in the great issues of document authority that the Internet introduces (how do you know the creator of the document is reliable, informed, or not crazy?) you end up with a very confusing situation. The long traditions of academic scholarship (peer review) are often obscured in the digital world. The seduction of the quick and dirty download is hard to resist, even for those who know better.

The best students and researchers will take these new tools, apply them intelligently and with perspective, and thereby extend their reach. Doing this is an art, and luckily that improves with time, intelligence and energy.

But research is so named because it is all about searching over and over again for the best stuff. The "re" in research suggests the thoroughness of the process— one search is never enough. The Internet and computers in general are capable of helping out here, and there are things that these technological tools do very well (word matching, sorting, and organizing) that really further scholarship.

But all tools need to be used with intelligence, even wisdom, and it is my hope that readers of this book will develop and extend their knowledge and critical faculties at the same time that they allow their curiosity to run over the wonderful world that we inhabit.

Good searching to you all.

Introduction

The Internet is a fabulous first date. It does not always make for a perfect marriage, but the promise offered at the first glimpse is enough to bring nearly everyone back for another look. Some of us, while not quite virtually married, nonetheless have established a long-term love affair with the Internet that allows for the recognition of its limitations and the less-than-perfect parts of the relationship. At times the temptation to grow frustrated with the insolence of the network, its insistence on absolutely perfect use of protocol and commands, is difficult to resist. Other times, while in the grasp of a particularly thorny problem, a colleague from across the country will send an email with the perfect solution, and all is forgiven. For many of us who were not originally trained in a computer environment, the idea of spending so much time in front of a television-like screen, dealing with what certainly appears to be simulated life, rather than the real reality we think we know so intimately, seems ludicrous and wasteful. The great books of the Middle Ages, whose illustrations and illuminations were carefully drawn by the hands of monks, possess a charm that seems irresistible after staring at the 97th Webpage of the day. Maybe the nay-sayers and traditionalists are right, and the Internet inhibits the deeper processes connected with the development of knowledge. Slow, creative, analytic thinking perhaps cannot be done in an electronic environment, but instead requires a long attention span and at least a temporary lull in the information saturation that characterizes our present society.

But the Internet has formed for me, and hopefully will for you, a delightful environment from which to extend one's interests. It offers information of all sorts, and can be used to locate statistical data, check when professional organizations are having their next conference (and sometimes register for them online), view images of ancient manuscripts, use library catalogs, check IRS rules for specific income tax questions, get the scoop on the latest article in an anthropology journal, and have fun socially corresponding with friends and colleagues and sharing the latest Internet jokes. The possibilities for education, entertainment, communication, and publication are nearly endless, and the subset of the Internet called the World Wide Web evolves daily and has taken on a life of its own that was impossible to envision even a few short years ago. The Internet mirrors our own life as humans—it reflects our passions and dedication, our attention to detail as well as our carelessness, our spite and malice, our need to reach out to others. It alternately aggravates and entices us, and while it may not be the answer to the problem of world hunger, it has the capacity to help in that effort, as well as many others. Like it or not, it is here to stay. It no longer is necessary to be a high-level scientist or computer expert to take part in it, and this book is designed to make its waters less forbidding and more comprehensible.

Most research cannot be limited solely to the use of Internet resources. For most major disciplines, the main corpus of knowledge continues to reside in books and journals. Especially at higher levels of research, the publications that define a given field will very likely not be available in a free electronic environment. While important papers and substantive research products have increasingly come to reside on individuals' Websites and various other locations, it is not now possible to regard this as a given. Generally the Internet will provide a "tip of the iceberg" view of important research, but it also offers a wide ability to locate and evaluate other resources for use.

At the same time, it would be foolish for a researcher in almost any discipline to ignore the development of Internet resources. At the very least the expansion and ease of communication is reason enough to consider the development of basic Internet navigational skills an important part of the toolkit that researchers use. Internet skills have been familiar for a great number of researchers for many years, notably in scientific and other technologically sophisticated disciplines, for whom the computer has long been a vital tool for research. Many other fields, notably in the humanities and social sciences, have been slower to accept the utility of online resources and the frustrating and tedious nature of learning unfamiliar skills.

Some Internet functions, following traditional research practice, work well over longer periods of time. Mailing lists serve to keep researchers current in their field by circulating current controversial topics and acting as forums for discussion. They can be invaluable for quick questions when the right resource is not at hand. Email itself is a vastly under-rated resource of the Internet, the most widely used of all the Internet functions. The right question directed to the right person can often save many hours of precious research time, and the speed of electronic communication is an unquestioned asset. Archives at FTP sites have long held unpublished papers and other valuable material, although it has not always been easy to locate that material. The rapid advances in Web browsers have opened avenues to self-publication of material that has been undoubtedly helpful, while at the same time potentially developing into an overwhelming avalanche of information.

The toughest problems connected with Internet resources have to do with evaluating the reliability of various resources and the disorganized state of information on the Internet. Many of the difficulties have been made easier to handle in recent years, and the current Web browsers simplify the commands necessary for a researcher unfamiliar with computer skills to operate effectively in an online environment. The kinds of skills mentioned in this book may either be nearly universal in a decade or completely out of date, but the process of research discussed herein will remain viable for a range of research tools and methods. In any event, it never hurts to be familiar with the framework and underpinning of network systems, since that understanding increases the functional basis of one's knowledge.

Many books currently residing in bookstores and libraries dealing with the Internet make it sound as if it was the greatest invention since Gutenberg's printing press. A smaller number suggest that no greater waste of time or lower common denominator of civilization has ever graced the face of the earth. For me the Internet is a marvelous tool for research. Using it effectively calls upon increased critical faculties, however. In the past, the academic tradition involved a model of apprenticeship, wherein the student worked under the supervision of a faculty member. Good methodology, sound grounding in the particular field's philosophical position, awareness of authoritative research — all were built into education. While the Internet represents a great growth of information generated by contemporary humans, and the potential for accessing impossible stretches of information is unprecedented, there is some danger of neglecting the traditional values inherent in the academic model. The need for critical analysis of resources has never been greater, but at the same time it is more difficult for the amateur to discern the nuances of excellent research. Further, in the electronic environment, where humans often represent themselves solely by the text they produce from a keyboard, the need for excellent writing skills is enormous. Yet the mechanisms to develop good communication skills are on shakier ground, at least in America. The traditional skills of the researcher — careful examination of resources, good analytic ability and excellent use of the written language — will continue to set good scholarship apart from lesser attempts.

This book is aimed at those who wish to take advantage of the Internet and Internet functions, to further their own research interests. It does not claim to be comprehensive, but more reflective of the ways that new tools can be utilized for more deeply ingrained research desires. It briefly discusses topics like Internet history, various Internet protocols, and techniques of online searching, areas that may be covered more exhaustively in other works with a more specific focus, many of which are mentioned in the bibliography. Readers are urged to extend their knowledge by using this work in combination with those of others dealing with more specific areas of Internet research. The epic proportions of all solid research — the struggles of finding resources, the attempts to evaluate the quality of the information, the battle to forge understanding out of the information uncovered, and the grueling process of crafting a final product, whether it be an oral presentation, a written paper or a thesis or dissertation — all are reflected in the use of the Internet as well.

The Internet is a community, a conduit for information, a collection of machines and their users, that defies comprehension. This book outlines the basic Internet protocols and explains how to use them. A lot of time is spent examining how Internet resources can be used for research. Looking for, finding, and evaluating information has become an activity of enormous consequence for us in our touted "information age." Besides specific Internet skills and resources, emphasis is placed on good research methods. I wish your own research efforts, in whatever form they take, the very best of luck.

1
System and
Knowledge Requirements

Basic Computer Skills

Computers as research tools have long been a part of the sciences and various other technologically advanced disciplines. However, for many people, computers are a relatively recent addition to their research toolkit. The dramatic decrease of computer prices and continued improvement in memory, speed, and processing power of home computers, combined with the explosion of interest in the Internet, has brought many first-time users to a computer. This lack of experience presents difficulties for many people, and these difficulties are compounded by the relative scarcity of convenient and effective methods for developing such skills.

Probably the best stance for new users to take is to realize that they must learn a new language. This learning involves a new vocabulary, a new grammar (the syntactical organization of computer commands), and last, but not least, an appreciation of computer culture. All these components are part of learning a new language, and as anyone who has gone through the initial stages of learning an unfamiliar language knows, the process is often a rocky and frustrating one. Additionally, a certain amount of practice is required, since there is a fairly high correspondence between effort and results.

Learning any new language, computer or otherwise, is not an easy proposition. Some elements of computer communication can defy even the most well-educated people. Fortunately, the minimum skills necessary to function in this new environment are not excessive, and software and hardware engineers are increasingly sensitive to the needs of new users. The continued development and use of Graphical User Interfaces (GUIs, pronounced "gooeys") has led to easier use of computers. It is no longer necessary to know cryptic commands to move or copy a file, start an application such as a word processing program, or otherwise manage a computer.

Unfortunately, it is often difficult to find good, precise documentation for using computers or for learning new applications. In most cases your best help will be found in third-party guides, which can be found in bookstores and libraries. Other courses of action include classes at community colleges or patient instruction from a willing colleague or fellow student.

Here are a few principles worth noting at this point if you want to develop any type of computer-related skill:

- *Be systematic*— Keep a notebook with problems, and remember to document difficult steps.

- *Be creative*— Often there is more than one way to accomplish a task.

- *Practice*— This is an obvious but critical component. Find real-world conditions that interest you and practice your skills. In my own classes the best results always occur when students take the concepts and skills they have just learned and immediately apply them to a task. This kind of learning is entirely akin to language acquisition — until you start speaking, the vocabulary and grammar exist only on a theoretical level, and it becomes difficult to move forward.

- *Be patient*— Chances are the worst that can happen is you end up losing some data. Try again, adding to your store of knowledge from your earlier mistakes.

- *Do not be afraid to ask*— Many people are willing to share their knowledge and expertise with you. Chances are excellent that you are not the first to encounter your particular problem.

The skills necessary to find your way around the Internet, both to move from site to site and to use the various basic Internet applications (Telnet, FTP, email), have not always been easy for people to master. Many functions at their most basic level (without a user-friendly interface such as Web browsers and other software provide) operate only one step removed from command language, which for many functions means UNIX operating system commands. UNIX is an operating system that was developed for powerful mainframe computers. It is also the most popular operating system for Internet servers. In the early days of the Internet, and until very recently, Internet users had to learn not only the operating system of their own computer, but many facets of the UNIX operating system as well. Today many of the GUI Internet applications used on personal computer platforms handle the UNIX operating system commands that need to be communicated to the Internet servers. However, a basic understanding of the UNIX operating system makes life much easier when using the Internet.

To make effective use of this book, you must be familiar with basic computer operation, including knowing how to turn on and run applications from your own computer. This obviously means functional knowledge of your operating system, be it an MS-DOS or Windows platform on a PC, or Mac OS on a Macintosh, or another workstation with a different operating system. There are many skills needed to navigate the Internet effectively above and beyond the skills necessary to operate a computer. There are many resources available, from books to classes, from which you can learn basic computer skills. For starters, you should know how to:

• Boot-up and shutdown your computer

• Launch an application

• Move and rename files

• Understand basic computer directory/folder and file structure

• Copy files from a floppy disk to your hard disk (and vice versa)

Basic Internet Skills

Internet functions are independent of the operating system software or hardware platform you use, but you still need to be able to find your way around your own workstation. It helps to remember that the differences in many Internet functions are due to either variations in the operating system being used on a particular computer or on the application being used to perform that function. There are many different software applications that can be used to send email, but sending an email message is conceptually the same whether you are using a PC with Windows 95, a Macintosh, or a UNIX workstation. However, the commands and actions you use may differ dramatically. Understanding the concept of what is actually taking place will make it easier to determine how the commands of your particular software package will perform a duty you know it can do.

In Chapter 3 each section on Internet functions will deal with specific concepts. The following section deals with general guidelines for Internet skill acquisition.

Internet Searching vs. Internet "Surfing"

Systematic searching is a quite different activity from Internet "surfing," which is a contemporary term for the casual browsing of material on the World Wide Web. Just as surfing in the ocean brings images of people riding wave after wave, surfing the Internet is riding wave after wave on the Internet, jumping from site to site looking at what this global network has to offer and probably finding valuable information in the process.

Using the Internet specifically as a research tool is something entirely different. Casually reading your local newspaper over the Internet is not research. Using the Internet to find resources to support a debate, write a report, develop a proposal, plan a presentation, or keep up on current issues in your field means using the Internet as a research tool. However, this does not mean that using the Internet for research cannot be fun.

Later in this chapter we will examine in detail the use of the Internet as part of the research process. However, there are some things you will need to know about the Internet and how it is arranged before you can begin to use it as a research tool.

Internet Addressing Conventions

The Internet is a network of interconnected networks all around the world. One computer is connected to a network, which is then connected to a larger network, which is then connected to an even larger network and so on.

Each and every computer on a network needs to have a unique identifier, much as your telephone number is unlike anyone else's. This identifier is referred to as a computer's address. If your computer is connected to the Internet, then it is using the TCP/IP communications protocol, and the address is called an IP (for Internet Protocol) address or Internet address. A computer on the Internet is also referred to as a host, server, or site. Computers can handle numbers faster than letters, so each IP address consists of four numbers, each less than 256, separated by periods, usually called "dots":

140.147.254.3

205.217.106.20

130.212.18.22

The hierarchy of networks in IP numbers reads from left to right. Each number represents a portion of a network, with each number to the right representing a smaller part of that network. The final number represents an individual computer on the network identified by the preceding numbers. Does this look confusing? Well, it does not to a computer. However, humans have developed a way to make it easier for you to remember Internet addresses: the Domain Name System (DNS).

DNS is a set of rules for naming computers using TCP/IP. Each computer is given a set of names, called domains, that correspond to a particular group. DNS names look similar to IP addresses but with letters instead of numbers (see Figure 1.1).

The final domain name in an addressing sequence is called a top-level domain (see Table 1.1). Each DNS address name can have up to four subdomain names and one top-level domain. The names are not completely intuitive, but it is still easier than remembering the numbers. Originally, there were six top-level domains: .com, .edu, .gov, .mil, .net, and .org.

The Internet has grown so large so quickly that the need for addresses has exceeded the capacity of the original top-level domain names, and new top-level domains are being registered constantly. Currently, there are over 250 top-level domains in use. The original six were primarily designed for businesses and institutions in the United States. Now there are two-letter codes for countries (see Table 1.2).

The hierarchy of DNS addresses reads from right to left, the opposite of how an IP address reads. Reading from right to left, each name represents a smaller network of computers. The leftmost name in an address represents an individual computer (see Figure 1.2).

All new second-level domains must be registered with one of the organizations that handle Internet names and keep track of sites and addresses (see http://www.internic.net/ for more information). Once a site has registered a top-level and at least one subdomain name, the site can then add computers within its domain. For example, if you register "mybiz.com," you can continue to add computers to your network giving them names like "number1.mybiz.com," "number2.mybiz.com," "number3.mybiz.

Figure 1.1 DNS syntax

Table 1.1 Top-level domains

Domain	Users	Example
.com	U.S. commercial businesses	ibm.com (International Business Machines)
.edu	U.S. educational institutions (universities, colleges, K–12, etc.)	harvard.edu (Harvard University)
.gov	U.S. nonmilitary government agencies and departments	whitehouse.gov (The White House)
.mil	U.S. military	army.mil (The U.S. Army)
.net	Network resources	internic.net (InterNIC— Network Information Center)
.org	Other organizations	greenpeace.org (the environmental group Greenpeace)

Table 1.2 Examples of two-letter country top-level domains

	Users	Example
.us	United States	sfpl.lib.ca.us (San Francisco Public Library)
.fr	France	senat.fr (French Senate)
.uk	United Kingdom	bbc.co.uk (British Broadcasting Company)
.jp	Japan	honda.co.jp (Honda — Japan)
.ru	Russia	mos.ru (Moscow Mayor's Office)
.au	Australia	unimelb.edu.au (University of Melbourne)

---

venus.sfsu.edu

venus

   is the name of the individual computer on the San Francisco State University network

sfsu

   represents the domain of the San Francisco State University network

edu

   represents the top-level domain of U.S. educational institutions

---

Figure 1.2 DNS hierarchy

com," and so on. Two computers can have the same name, as long as they are not under the same top-level domain.

The numerical IP addresses are still used, but the numbers are "transparent" (or invisible) to the user for the most part. For example, if you enter the address for the Library of Congress online catalog, which is locis.loc.gov, a computer translates that into 140.147.25.3 so that you do not need to know the numerical IP address.

Identifying Internet Addresses

Just as every computer on a network must have a unique address, every user of that network must also have a unique identifier. When you select an Internet service provider (ISP), you will be given an account with that provider's network. Usually, you will be asked to select a name for your account. This name is called a username or login name. A username and an Internet computer address, usually a domain name, constitute your unique identifier on the Internet. It is also your Internet email address.

If you have access to a network and email at work, your email address at work may or may not be an Internet email address. Internet addresses follow a specific syntax defined for the TCP/IP protocol. Different network protocols, such as Novell, Windows NT, and others, may use a different syntax for identifying email addresses. It is possible to send and receive Internet email from a non–TCP/IP network. Check with your network administrator for more information.

Internet email addresses follow a specific syntax. The number of subdomains in an Internet email address may vary, but at least one is required.

Email addresses on the Internet are not always for individual people. It is possible for a department or a division or a company to have an email address. This is done mainly for convenience. It is easier to write to info@microsoft.com than to locate the individual email address of a particular employee.

Figure 1.3 Internet email address syntax

Using the Uniform Resource Locator (URL)

When you refer someone to an article in a newspaper or magazine, you want to give that person all the information necessary to locate that article. This type of referral is called a citation. A typical citation for an article may look like this:

> Miller, David. 1994. "The Many Faces of the Internet." *Internet World* 5, no. 7 (October): 34.

This citation gives the reader the author's name, date of publication, title of the article, title of the magazine, volume number, issue number, month of publication, and page number. There are several different standards for citations (see Appendix B), but the primary purpose for citing references is to document your research so that your readers may follow your work.

On the Internet, there is a standard for referring to electronic information, especially when referring to it in written form. It is simply not good enough to refer to "the New York Public Library site" or "the weather site." This standard is called a URL, or a Uniform Resource Locator. URLs are everywhere on the Internet and they will be presented throughout this book, so it is important that you understand their meaning and appearance. Once you know how to interpret URLs, navigating the Internet becomes much easier.

URLs can be used to refer to any type of document on the Internet and the type of access to that document. By access we are referring to the application protocol you must use to locate the document that is being represented. There are several different Internet application protocols such as Telnet, FTP, SMTP (email), and others; each is discussed in detail in Chapter 3.

The syntax, or arrangement, of a URL is as follows:

<scheme>:<scheme-dependent-information>

A scheme refers to the type of Internet application protocol. Scheme-dependent-information includes the Internet machine address and any directory or file information necessary to locate a document.

A basic URL might look like this:

http://www.cnn.com/US/index.html

This example is for a World Wide Web document. The "http" scheme refers to HyperText Transfer Protocol, the standard that controls the transfer of documents on the World Wide Web (WWW). The scheme is followed by a colon (:) and a double forward slash (//), which begins the scheme-specific information. In this case the machine address is www.cnn.com, the WWW site for CNN, the Cable News Network. The directory and file information is /US/index.html, which indicates that the document being referred to is index.html and is located in the US directory. This document is the index page for U.S. news of the day.

There are additional URL scheme names, but the ones in Table 1.3 are the most common found on the Internet.

URLs can also be used to direct software to particular sites on the Internet. A WWW application, for example, will automatically interpret a URL beginning with "http://" as a Web document and go to that address and retrieve the document. Depending upon your software configuration, URLs may be interpreted automatically and the correct software application launched.

Prior to the use of URLs, instructions for using resources on the Internet looked like this:

Telnet to "delocn.udel.edu" and login as "info," but do not type in the quotation marks.

This type or representation presented problems in written form because there was no standard for including things like quotation marks, commas, periods, and other English punctuation. Now that same information can be represented as

telnet://info:delocn.udel.edu

Table 1.3 Internet application protocols and their URL scheme names

Application Protocol	URL scheme name	Example
HyperText Transfer Protocol	http	http://www.cnn.com
File Transfer Protocol	ftp	ftp://ftp.apple.com
Gopher Protocol	gopher	gopher://gopher.ucsc.edu
Electronic Mail	mailto	mailto:info@microsoft.com
Usenet News	news	news:misc.health.diabetes
Telnet	telnet	telnet://sfpl.lib.ca.us
Wide Area Information Search	wais	wais://cnidr.org

URLs provide a standard way for you to locate or refer to an electronic resource or document. This avoids the confusion that may arise when someone says "Connect to the Library of Congress." There are several different meanings for the word "connect" on the Internet. With the many application protocols used on the Internet, URLs provide a way of representing the correct protocol for a particular document or resource.

2
The Nature of Research

The Research Process

Research, the locating and synthesis of information into meaningful understanding, is something that all of us do, often without realizing it. As humans we are constantly asking questions and wondering about things, a quality that is a hallmark of our species. This curiosity often then prompts us to try to find answers. We locate information with an astonishingly wide range of methods: we ask other people; we read books, journal articles, and newspapers; we dig into reference books, archives of birth records, company financial reports, and our own file drawers. Sometimes we just need one little fact to put our understanding in the correct place. Other times one question leads to another, and before we know it, we have bitten off a big study. Reality has a habit of being more complicated than it appears and it never hurts to remember this when "doing research."

Research methods vary somewhat, depending on what one's topic or interests are, but there are some common elements to all research that are worth noting. In many cases, others have come before you, looking for exactly the same information you are looking for. This means, sometimes, that they have already done some of your work for you, but that does not mean that you cannot uncover something new. The following path, which applies to all research, from great to small, is one model of the research process:

Step 1. Define your topic
Step 2. Identify useful sources
Step 3. Locate information
Step 4. Evaluate information
Step 5. Analyze information
Step 6. Synthesize information
Step 7. Document your research

The following is a graphical representation of the research process, moving from the top down, which is never as simple as this model suggests. Each step is likely to loop back to the previous step so that information evaluation leads back to another round of locating resources, etc. This book is directed to the steps listed to the right of the line. We address the identification, location, and evaluation of resources and their documentation for the creation of the final product. Topic definition and the analysis and synthesis phases are largely the result of your own training in your particular discipline, the places where you bring your intelligence, creativity, and overall intellectual abilities to bear on the topic of choice.

Topic Definition

$\qquad$ Identify Useful Resources

Locate Information

Evaluate Information

Analyze information

Synthesize information

Document your research

Finished Product

Selecting and Defining a Research Topic

Selecting and defining a topic is often the hardest part of any research project, and good preparation is important. If the selection and definition of a topic is done well, the rest of the process is considerably easier.

What exactly do you want to know? What is missing in your understanding? What are the requirements for your project? The more you can develop a clearly defined question or set of questions, the easier it is to locate and use the information you will consider. This can be difficult if you have only a vague idea of what you need or want. Whatever you can do to more clearly sculpt the nature of your topic may prove most helpful in your journey.

As a student, often your research projects are chosen for you by your professor. In this case he or she is your primary audience, and your project must be tailored to his or her standards. Other times you are given latitude for a range of topic choices and must decide what to study and how great or small to make your arena of interest. At work you may be assigned a project, and your efforts must contribute to the good of the organization.

Often your initial interest can be so hopelessly large that initial research seems daunting. Any study about the American Civil War involves a consideration of a huge body of knowledge. Are there specific aspects of your topic you are particularly interested in? A region (Virginia?), an aspect (economic?), a technology (railroad transportation?), or a person (Stonewall Jackson?)? A recent search of the Internet for the phrase "civil war" retrieved over 700,000 records. Focusing on a small, clearly defined part of the whole may speed your efforts and result in more gratifying results with less irrelevant material to get in your way.

Broad topics are not useless, but they can quickly become ineffective when searching large databases such as you will find on the Internet. Finding too much information can be as frustrating as finding no information. You should always start with a broad topic that can be narrowed down to a more specific research question.

Your research topic may become so narrowly defined that you end up finding very little information. When this happens, the same kind of tricks you use to narrow your topic can be used to broaden it: identifying keywords and selecting alternative terms.

The important thing to remember for the process of defining a topic is that time spent thinking out exactly what it is you want will pay off in the process and in the product. As with many other things in life, the clearer the goals, the greater the chance of their attainment.

Identifying Useful Resources

The nature of your inquiry also determines the extent and quality of your resources. If your topic is a high-level, in-depth study of a psychological theory, a general interest magazine such as *Time* will not be an appropriate resource except perhaps to gather ideas and names. Instead, an academic journal will be more appropriate.

You should always keep in mind your intended audience. Are you presenting your findings before the board of directors of your organization? Are the results for you alone? Who is likely to see or benefit from your findings? What will the format be — paper, talk, or email message?

If the results are purely for your own edification, you are the one to determine what will be satisfactory (and satisfying). Otherwise, the effect and utility of your findings will to a large degree be measured by how well you know and understand your audience. What do they view as authoritative resources? Do they read *Newsweek* or *The Journal of Psychiatric Care*? By pitching your results to the appropriate level of understanding of your audience, you will be better prepared to communicate effectively with that audience. Your own credibility is heightened when others can see how systematic you have been and how carefully you have considered the issue and the available resources.

Resources are basically of two types: primary and secondary. They differ in the amount of interpretation or analysis contributed by the person who developed them. Primary sources consist of statistics, eyewitness accounts, various archival materials (such as birth records and vehicle registrations), survey results, measurements of a widely varied nature (time, temperature, size, weight, etc.), and different types of written records, including diaries and chronicles. For nearly all high-level research, and often in general, primary resources are preferred.

Secondary sources involve reflective consideration of various primary source material by a person or persons. They exist as books, journal or magazine articles, opinion pieces in newspapers, prepared reports, and television documentaries. Secondary sources are interpretative; they are the result of analysis. The line between primary and secondary sources is sometimes blurred, but the main distinction is the amount of reflective thought used in the preparation of the work. An example of the difference between primary resources and secondary resources is this: The novel *Gravity's Rainbow* by Thomas Pynchon is a primary resource. It is a creative work, original and unique. An article analyzing this novel in the 1992 issue of the journal *Critique* and written by Kathryn Hume is a secondary source because it is written by another person who has interpreted the novel, a primary source, in a particular fashion. Additionally, 1990 census data for the state of New York is a primary resource, but a projection of population growth according to age or ethnicity would be a secondary source because it would involve an interpretation and extrapolation of the census data.

In general, primary sources require more original thought, and using them may require a great deal of sifting. Secondary sources are interpretations by various scholars and others, and constitute the bulk of books and journals. Either or both types of resources may be appropriate for your own study.

Identifying your resources is closely tied to your first step of topic definition, and the two may influence each other. Sometimes they occur in parallel, and to gather ideas for a topic it may be necessary to skim the information resources available to see what is potentially useful. The nature of your inquiry may determine for you what sorts of resources to use, and some of the definition will derive from your own experience. If you are concerned with a current affairs topic, newspapers may be the most appropriate resource to utilize. If you are interested in the latest biological research, a scholarly or academic journal is probably the best place to look. Often one resource will lead to another, either by mention in the body of the material or in a footnote or bibliography. An obvious and often extremely helpful step is to consult with someone more familiar than you with your topic or area. Assisting people with research is the job of reference librarians around the world. In addition, instructors and practicing professionals in your area of interest are often willing to share their knowledge and enthusiasm.

Locating Information

Once you have a fairly clear idea of what you want to know and what kinds of resources might be helpful to you, the process of rounding up the informative material may then begin. What you need will determine where to go looking for it. One of the great advantages of electronic searching is remote access. With remote access one can sift through and evaluate a lot of material regardless of where that material is physically housed. As we will see in the section on remote access, you can browse the Internet for resources. Part of this is simply convenient: you can check the catalog of your local library to see if a particular item is checked out before you go across town to pick it up. However, depending on your topic, it may be possible to retrieve the material right to your own workstation, without leaving your home or office.

Locating material can present peculiar challenges, however, and your topic may be one that is difficult to penetrate. On the Internet there exists a myriad of resources, both professionally and individually produced, that may assist you in your research. Commercial information services such as DIALOG and IAC (Information Access Company) make a business of keeping large databases of available information in a well-organized fashion, grouping lists of newspaper articles, journal articles, government documents, and conference papers in useful categories. These databases are available by subscription, but the cost is usually beyond most individuals' means or needs. However, many college and university libraries have for several years made these commercial databases available to students and faculty, and an increasing number of public libraries are also making these databases available to their patrons.

There are also many "free" databases available on the Internet. "Free" because nothing is ever really free of costs. You do have to have an Internet connection in order to access Internet databases, but once you have that connection, use of the databases is available at no extra charge. We will look more closely at these kinds of resources in the section on online searching, for there are different types of databases and different methods of searching them.

The locating phase of the research process can actually incorporate several steps. An index can help identify the material that might be useful. A second step is the retrieval of that information, which may involve determining where the material is housed (a library, bookstore, archive, Internet site, etc.).

Retrieval of the material often presents its own set of logistical problems, which is one reason why starting your research early is beneficial, since it allows time for extended retrieval or evaluation of resources. Not long ago, locating a source that turned out to be across the country or further presented a difficult situation. In present-day libraries the Interlibrary Loan service (often available free or at a minimal charge at libraries) allows your local library to borrow books and journal articles from other libraries and check them out to you. Obviously, there is a range of material, particularly rare books and archival material, that may not be available this way, but one should never rule out a resource merely because of its distant location. If the resource is local, then the retrieval issues are simpler. Even those not affiliated with a college or university library can often arrange borrowing privileges (usually for a fee). Journal articles often can be photocopied if not actually withdrawn from a library.

As we will explore later in the book, certain resources, notably government information, lend themselves very well to remote electronic retrieval, and it is often a good thing to realize the resources that can be reached electronically as one conducts this phase of the research process.

In whatever manner the location and retrieval end of the process takes place, it is often necessary to loop back into the first and second phases of the research process. Getting some material often prompts further questions that you had not identified earlier. One person's work ends up being so useful that you want to explore more of his or her efforts. All of this falls into the evaluation phase.

Evaluating Information

The evaluation phase is one of the hardest to perfect, and it causes problems even for experienced researchers. How do you know if the material you have gathered will answer all of your questions? All sorts of issues present themselves. Is the material current and reflective of contemporary thinking on the topic? Are the authors well respected in their field? Are there contrary perspectives missing or needed? How do I know when to stop looking for more material?

Some of these difficulties can be handled by careful framing of the first part of the process. The more clearly the research goals are formulated, the easier it is to place the research need into the framework of current research efforts. If needs are more modest, then many of the worries are less annoying, although in many fields currency of information is crucial. This phase can be particularly difficult if one is unfamiliar with the field. One must decide how deep one needs to dig, for to be exhaustive may exceed time limits and other project boundaries.

In the world of academic research, there are several clues to whether your sources are good ones:

- *Kind of publication*— Scholarly journals are usually the medium of choice for high-level research. The latest and most in-depth research on schizophrenia or genetics will not appear in *Time* or *Newsweek* but in journals devoted to professional research in the field.

- *Format*— Footnotes and a bibliography are clues to well-prepared resources. An absence of them may indicate a lack of research rigor.

- *Credentials of the author*— Is the author connected with a college or university? A CEO of a company or a marketing representative? How do you know the opinions voiced are not those of a garrulous windbag? Complete lack of identification, unless there is a clear reason for anonymity, is a real problem because there is no accountability at all.

- *Logical consistency*— This can be a difficult concept, but it remains a useful clue to the worth of a source. Does the material hold up to your own analysis? Are the arguments clearly constructed and well documented? Does the emotional tone of the author overshadow the content? There is often room for a sound argument on a particular issue, even if some of the other attributes (credentials for example) are missing. What will your intended audience think of this? There is no point in using a resource that is going to be dismissed by your audience unless you are prepared to demonstrate, very clearly and convincingly, why it is valuable.

Analysis and Synthesis

The analysis phase is an individualized phase. This is where you analyze all the resources you have gathered and decide, for yourself, if they meet your needs. You make conclusions about what you have gathered. If you have clearly defined your research topic, identified and gathered useful sources of material, and evaluated that material for clarity, credentials, and relevancy, you can now begin to analyze the information in an effort to incorporate it into an end-product. This product could be a paper, a report, a presentation, or simply an answer to a question you have posed to your-self.

The synthesis phase is when you incorporate what you have learned into your body of knowledge and use it. Depending on your research needs, you will need to develop an understanding that you can communicate to others. The clarity of your understanding and the importance of the resources will make a big difference in the impact your efforts have. Your skills in written or spoken language and graphic representation, as well as your energy and thoroughness, all come to bear.

Documentation

Here it is your own thinking that produces the result of all that you have uncovered, whether it be a report, a presentation, or just a heightened understanding with which to further your own quest.

This final stage of the process must not be minimized. Your audience will appreciate the ways that you have identified your resources and out-lined your path of thinking. You should not be overly possessive of your resources. By clearly indicating your list of resources in a bibliography or footnotes (or in a handout after an oral presentation) you strengthen your own position, and your audience will appreciate your organization and attention to detail. Good analysis is strengthened if the results can be dupli-cated by another (this is a key element of the sciences, where conclusions drawn from an experiment are suspect if they cannot be duplicated by other scientists following up by doing similar experiments).

One part of your documentation, at least at higher levels of research, is a meticulously prepared list of sources. It is frequently necessary to use a style manual or particular format for listing resources (for example, psy-chology research uses a style developed by the American Psychological Asso-ciation). These style manuals illustrate conventions shared by the group to standardize the information listed. We will examine style manuals in more detail in the appendix on citation, but you need to be aware of the neces-sity of their use in the documentation of your research. A typical example of a citation in the "*Chicago s*tyle" looks like this:

Krol, Ed. *The Whole Internet User's Guide & Catalog.* 2d ed. Sebastopol, Calif.: O'Reilly, 1994.

Traditionally, the author is listed first, achieving primacy for the creation of the work. The title follows, then facts of publication (city, publisher, and date for books; volume, issue, and date for periodicals), and then page numbers.

Research Problems

Research is rarely an easy proposition. If it were, everyone would be doing it and making piles of money off of the activity. Good research calls for several qualities, not all of them related.

Unfortunately, research methodology tends to be taught systematically only at the highest levels of university study. Methodology courses are often a key part of graduate study where the research tools utilized by the chosen discipline, whether they be statistical, textual, etc., are discussed and employed. Research theory tends to be a topic severely neglected before then. Many high school and college students feel that research is something they should know how to do, but formal education in this area usually is erratic.

Problems in conducting research break into several areas, but the first one is paramount — lack of a theoretical framework. Without suitable concepts to remedy this lack, the best approach is to study the often meager literature on the topic and then begin empirical work yourself. Research always begins with an inquiring mind, however, and possession of one improves results at every stage of the process.

Essential qualities in the researcher include:

- *Inquisitiveness*— The launching pad for all research is a curious mind.

- *Information-gathering skills*— We will examine at length this part of the research process. It is perhaps the most "learnable" of all research qualities.

- *Analytic and synthetic abilities*— These vary from discipline to discipline. Humanities researchers are apt to employ methods far different from biologists. But any good researcher possesses the ability to make connections amidst a range of data and to generalize a set of conclusions from a particular sample.

- *Careful attention to detail*— This is needed both in the gathering of information and in its analysis and documentation. Carelessness in any of these phases weakens your conclusions and gives critics an opportunity to argue against your insights.

- *Communication*— This ability too is easily learned, and its importance should not be minimized. A good argument suffers if poorly presented, and many a worthy point has been discredited because of the weakness of its presentation.

Before throwing up your hands at this impossible list of requirements, remember that humans exhibit all these qualities in daily life and that all are hallmarks of our problem-solving species. All day long we are involved in activities that demand we pay attention, locate solutions to problems, and communicate with our fellow workers, friends, and families. Many of these behaviors are adaptable to research environments, and all of them can be developed.

Inquisitiveness

At some point in his or her life, every researcher has had the difficulty of developing a topic. The area of interest can be so broad as to appear overwhelming. Or it can be so narrowly focused that extracting enough data to make a meaningful study seems impossible. Solutions for these problems can come from several directions. Topic definition can often be prompted by a literature review. Read the background sources. Find similar problems that have been dealt with by others in the field. How did they proceed? What questions were posed? Is there any way to adapt these questions to your own area of interest? When thinking of a topic, think of ways to express that interest in a question.

Often when you are completely stumped, it makes sense to review what others have written about your area of interest or even about areas that appear to be related. Thoughtful review of secondary sources may prompt you to generate questions of your own. Sometimes it is possible to apply a perspective or approach that worked in one distinct area to another.

Information-Gathering Skills

Data is the core of research. Not enough and you just plain cannot proceed. What to do to gather more? Is the lack of data a result of your inability to locate data from anyone else's work? Is the area just one that has not been studied to any great degree? Or is there so much data out there that it proves impossible to decide what to look at? Are you overwhelmed?

This part of the research process can be an infinite loop. In fact, it should probably loop more than once for the results to be superior. Rarely is an inquiry posed so perfectly that there is not another way to phrase it or another perspective to take.

The standard approach is to reexamine the way the topic has been framed. If your retrieval set is extremely large, is it possible to focus your interest more narrowly? If extremely small, perhaps there is a way to describe your interest that will include it in a broader field of study. Perhaps your particular interest tends to be included only in works of a broader nature. The search terms can also be problems and may not reflect your real interests. The standard advice here is to consult a listing of terms used to describe the topic. Most college and university libraries have a multivolume set of Library of Congress subject headings, which lists the terms employed by library catalogs to organize subject material. Browsing this list can help define one's interest or suggest alternative terms to use in a search. Certain disciplines, such as medicine, have their own extremely precise subject terms (Mesh or Medical Subject Headings) that may be essential for good results in a search.

Another strategy is to assume the stance "the first one is the hardest one" when thinking of locating material and to cast a broad net, recognizing that a lot of sifting may have to take place to get that first "good" item. Once you have found such an item, one that seems to reflect your own interest well, there are several paths to take. By examining the catalog record, it is often possible to find additional subject headings that perhaps escaped your attention earlier. Using them to conduct another search may allow you to home in on your topic in its particular niche. Additionally, you may want to examine the other works of the author(s), who may have written more extensively on the topic or other related subjects. Once you have the item in hand, it is usually useful to examine the bibliography or footnotes because they will direct you to other material.

Analysis and Synthesis

The analytic phase is also an easy place to get stuck. As you attempt to decipher the meaning in your mountain of data, the size and unwieldy nature of your collection may be overwhelming. How have other researchers dealt with similar kinds of data? Sometimes methods for one discipline may be applied to another, especially if the data set is unusual in some fashion. Although this strategy must be used with caution, since most disciplines have developed their unique methods for a reason, it can often suggest different ways to view the data. Increasingly, for example, researchers are finding biological models that help explain areas normally considered to be quite divergent from biological concerns, such as computers and physics.

Often it is helpful to begin writing up your conclusions before you feel you have entirely digested your data set. This can allow you to look critically at what you are proposing and decide if your data clearly support your findings. Are you going out on a limb at all? There may be good reasons to do so, but it is best if you find ways to support the weight of your results. Talk your results up with others in the field, or even with non-specialist friends or colleagues who might provide some interesting questions or different perspectives.

Attention to Detail

Whatever it takes for you to stay organized in your efforts is worth doing. Many methods of storing and organizing searches, data, and thoughts exist, and they range from keeping a simple notebook to the creation and maintenance of computer files. Find a method that works for you, and include as much relevant material in it as you think necessary (maybe even more). Review it regularly, and do not be afraid to rearrange things. Sometimes a different order of data can prompt a new view.

Communication

Communication of your findings is usually regarded as the final product of research, the polished result of your efforts. As such, it should be thorough and logically consistent. You are the guide to the reader (or listener), and your role is to take your audience along to witness your evidence and think along with you. It makes sense to set the framework for your inquiry in broad terms because not everyone in your audience will be as familiar as you with the topic. To communicate well you not only need a firm grasp of your chosen language but an ability to anticipate the interests and reactions of your intended audience. The first can never suffer from too much practice, and good speaking and writing skills are essential and can always be improved. It may take some imagination on your part to reflect on the mindset of your audience, but doing so will help you organize your product to maximize its effect.

As noted earlier, however, communication can also help in shaping the path your research takes at earlier stages. Contacting other people with interests in your area can spark new approaches and ideas. How you communicate about your interest usually reflects how you have organized it in your own thinking. By viewing your provisional results, you get an opportunity to rethink your structure.

Research problems can lead to real insight. It is often helpful to remember that a neat, linear line towards success is rare and that the actual process of extending one's understanding through the locating and digesting of resource material is a worthy journey, even when results are minimal.

The Internet as a Research Tool

The first stage of research remains the same, regardless of the type of equipment (computer or otherwise) used to conduct it: the researcher must determine the needs of the project, whether it be finding a simple fact or doing extensive study on a complex topic. Before the Internet or any other resource can be utilized, it helps to have a clear idea about what is necessary. The Internet should be considered, and evaluated, the same as any other kind of resource at hand.

As a research tool the Internet operates in two ways. First, it permits wider, faster, and easier access to much information that already exists. For example, bulletins put out by the United States Department of Agriculture (USDA) have long been widely distributed to libraries that house government documents, and any library visitor could consult them. The Internet makes it possible to access those bulletins remotely, regardless of time or distance considerations, and the documents can be downloaded and studied at the user's convenience. Second, the Internet simplifies the process of self-publication so that new information can be made more widely available. In this sense a truly new body of information is created, and much potentially valuable research material that previously might not have been accessible is out in the world for examination.

This twofold development creates some problems for researchers, however. The existence of information is not useful if it cannot be found. Usually, for most things, more is better, but if more information creates problems of location and retrieval, as it often does on the Internet, then progress is not always an improvement.

For evaluating information, our first example does not pose particular problems. If the USDA puts out a bulletin, its authority is identical whether the file is electronic or on paper, and the agency's reputation is based on a long-standing and highly visible track record. In the second case, where new information is presented, the authority and value of the information is more difficult to ascertain. With self-publication so easy to accomplish, all sorts of drivel can be put up in no time. How are you to know if what you are examining is solid information? We will return to this very pressing problem shortly.

What Is Available on the Internet

The Internet allows access to a wide range of research material, including both primary and secondary resources. All kinds of organizations make their data available on the Internet, ranging from federal and local governments to research and professional societies, museums, schools, and electronic archives. There are electronic journals, political party agendas, and, increasingly, marketing and advertising material.

Although it would be a mistake to use only the Internet in the research process, thereby ignoring a wealth of other material (often much better organized), for some kinds of research it is invaluable. Some of the issues a researcher must grapple with are how exhaustive the research process is planned to be, the characteristics of the intended audience, and the nature of the presentation of the research.

The Internet has some very clear advantages for certain kinds of research. These include:

- *Wide range of access*— Many resources can be reached from your own computer. You are able to view paintings, read manuscripts, and browse through library collections that may be continents away without the usual limitations of time and distance.

- *Immediate retrieval*— Resources can be viewed on your own computer, where you can examine them or save them to your own hard drive for later and a closer examination. The Internet is "open" 24 hours a day, seven days a week.

- *Variety of formats*— Information can be transferred over the Internet in various formats: text, images, sound, video, and animation.

- *Currency* — Many Internet resources are updated very quickly and often represent the latest available information.

- *Human communication* — For surveys and other kinds of data gathering that depend on human respondents, the communication power of the Internet can be extremely attractive.

The Internet, however, is not the final answer to research. Some of its drawbacks include:

- *Uncertain reliability*— One of the hidden but valuable aspects of a library or other traditional resource repository is that the collection of material has been selected carefully. Careless research or ill-conceived works are generally not selected in favor of important works that will stand the rigors of time and continued reflection. The Internet makes it so easy to disseminate information that the real value of the material is sometimes difficult to gauge.

- *Questionable credibility*— The Internet allows for nearly anyone to publish content. Although this is certainly the most democratic and effective means of allowing all voices to be heard, much of the information available on the Internet has little or no credibility.

- *Disorganization*— Despite the valiant efforts of companies that endeavor to create searching mechanisms for locating Internet resources, Internet organization remains chaotic, with few of the highly evolved classification frameworks displayed by libraries and archives. This disorganization increases the need for good online searching skills. In addition, research has always been a time-intensive process with the need to forage continually for new or better information. Searching Internet resources can be time consuming and sometimes less productive than the use of more traditional resources.

- *Ethical issues* — Because material is made so available and in a form that may be appropriated so easily, the temptation to use that material without citation or without regard to copyright considerations is much greater than with traditional material.

- *Heightened expectations*— With the explosive growth of the Internet into public consciousness and the resultant expansion of the volume of information being made available, it is easy to think that you may find anything and everything on the Internet. This sort of thinking can easily cloud good evaluation skills during research and cause you to ignore other resources that might be more valuable to your work simply because they are not available on the Internet.

Despite these drawbacks there are aspects of Internet research that extend the range of the researcher's arm. Several kinds of research can be particularly well served by including Internet resources.

With advances developed by the latest software and hardware technology, a variety of sights and sounds can greet the researcher, along with the written text that has traditionally held sway. Although viewing a digitized image of the *Mona Lisa* does not compare even remotely with seeing it in person, it still allows insight that is not possible by mere textual description alone. Subjects like art and biology, which benefit from visual aids, or any projects that involve blueprints or plans, pictures or drawings, are good candidates for the use of Internet resources, as are all types of information needing to be distributed widely and quickly.

Current Information

Various kinds of information that depend on currency — for example, statistics, marketing, or other business-related information — are often well served in an Internet environment. Certain kinds of facts, including airline schedules and international rates of currency exchange, are available on the Internet, but others, particularly if they represent sensitive or proprietary interests, may not be so easily available. Often this sort of information is held by proprietary companies in the business of brokering information, such as the LEXIS-NEXIS news service or Westlaw in legal matters. Depending on one's interests, it may be extremely worthwhile to spend the money to have an account with one of these services because their information impact can be so great.

It is possible to subscribe to a kind of "current awareness service" that will alert you to news releases on hot topics of your choice or even perform a search for you and send you the results daily via email. In this sense the Internet provides a way for you to remain current on topics of personal interest.

Information About Organizations

A huge array of businesses, educational, and governmental organizations have seen the value of making information about themselves available to anyone with a computer able to reach them. Businesses have an enormous stake in the World Wide Web as a marketing tool, but the information posted there must be seen in light of its intended purpose (marketing) and may not necessarily replace a good reference resource found in a library. Still, for facts about the company, such as address, officers, and other background material, the Internet works very well. Nonprofit organizations and research centers are finding the Internet to be an efficient way to post information about their work. This is true of governmental and educational organizations as well. Every U.S. federal agency has an Internet presence of some sort, even the IRS and the CIA. Colleges and universities increasingly make available their catalogs and course descriptions, as well as providing means to communicate with various people and offices on campus.

Research That Involves Communication

If your interests involve surveys or the gathering of data from respondents, the communication advantages of the Internet can be extremely valuable. Plenty of kinds of data gathering still depend on face-to-face or immediate contact, and many important social scientists still prefer this method,

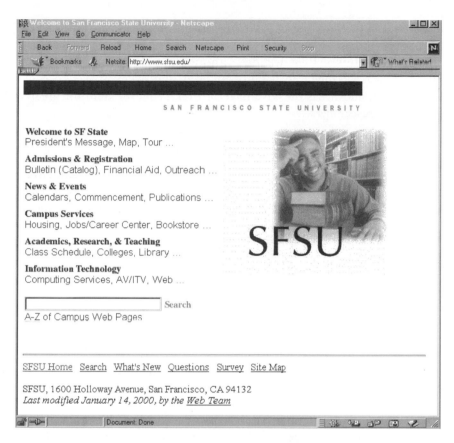

San Francisco State University Homepage — an example of an organization's homepage with topic organization and hyperlinks. (Copyright ©1998 San Francisco State University.)

even when the topic might be related to the Internet itself, but various kinds of research benefit from the ease and range of email. If your interests necessitate the frequent posing of questions or sharing of manuscripts or other kinds of documents, the Internet can be extremely valuable. Parts of the first edition of this book were written at a variety of places, and my coauthor and I were able to share our created work in progress to edit and perform other processes that would have been slowed had we had to exchange physical manuscripts.

Rare or Hard-to-Reach Resources

Many artifacts and manuscripts are too valuable to be made easily available in museums or libraries. Age, fragility or extreme value may discourage casual viewing or handling. If digitized and accompanied by text, many of these sorts of items are increasingly being made available to those with an Internet connection. Although not always a substitute for actual contact, this digital availability can be an improvement over no availability at all, and it has the advantage of preserving the item for greater numbers of researchers.

Manipulation of Data

Various kinds of research may involve manipulation of data, either graphically or textually, and the resources that can be retrieved and used at one's own computer are invaluable for certain kinds of analysis. Although having a book in hand is preferable for most kinds of analysis, a review of the use and frequency of certain word occurrences can be accomplished easily and efficiently when that document exists in electronic form. As computer skills become more and more a part of the body of skills possessed by researchers, this sort of manipulation and analysis will grow increasingly important.

Evaluation of Internet Information

The problems of evaluation exist to an unusual degree when considering the use of Internet resources. There are vast difficulties pertaining to resource reliability — the accuracy and validity of the information presented. These issues, although hardly absent, are less problematic for most traditional resources. Location of resources can be particularly troublesome when the resource material is unpublished, perhaps a set of conference proceedings. Additionally, in all research the integrity of the resource material is of paramount importance, but the tradition of research in academic and other arenas has built a framework of professionalism that is more identifiable than in the world of the Internet.

Address Stability

Unfortunately, the fluid nature of electronic resources, which is one of their advantages, also contributes to a nomadic placement. Files that one day were stored on stargazer.umissouri.edu may migrate to another machine, often for reasons that are not made explicit and usually without any way of your knowing that this has happened. Suppose you are a systems administrator at the University of Missouri and have been holding the complete collections of Mark Twain on one of your university computers. Disk space has become more valuable for a number of reasons, and you are looking for ways to maximize your limited hardware resources. Perhaps it is advantageous to move the large files to a different machine. Or maybe you have realized that the University of Minnesota also holds copies of the files and that the reasons for duplicating their archives are not strong enough to justify the use of your own disk space. These and dozens of other reasons may produce the result of "files here today, gone tomorrow." Conscientious systems operators may have the opportunity and inclination to leave a message at the old address, pointing to a new and different address, but this does not always happen. Gopher sites were notorious for continual juggling of resource locations, and the growth of the Web has made the problems even greater.

Web sites come and go with startling abruptness, but the Internet community is not oblivious to the problems. One movement afoot at the moment is to develop mechanisms for a file to automatically list its new address at the site of its old address, somewhat like the forwarding information requested by the U.S. Postal Service when an individual moves to a new home. When standardized and made universal, this practice will go a long way toward improving the reliability of location of resources.

Visiting a site that once housed some precious information and discovering that it is gone (and not knowing why) is not a comfortable feeling. One helpful practice is to be meticulous in your own documentation of the resources, to the extent of reading README files of the site, which provide content and organizational information about the site, to have some advance warning of coming changes. Having a careful list of files and locations that you have visited in your research also minimizes the times when you have doubts yourself about whether you have come to the right place or not. If your record clearly states an accurate address and a date, you can then feel confident that the files have moved and not just that you cannot find them because of some lack on your part. Knowing how to use some of the search engines also enables you to find the material if in fact it has moved somewhere else.

Resource Authority

What makes for reliable information? A primary concern is trust. Are the person or persons who created the information accurate and honest? In the academic and professional world, a series of safeguards and conventions helps assure reliable research. Peer review, the process by which a profession or discipline examines the current scholarship generated by the peer group, serves to scrutinize research results and reject research findings that are careless, poorly analyzed, or exceed the boundaries of respected professionalism. This in no way assures a homogeneous product from a given profession, and in fact nearly every active discipline is rife with intellectual argument over methods, findings, attention to detail, and experimental bias. Peer review does tend to raise the common denominator of the research to the highest possible level, however, and encourages rigorous research procedures among all members of a profession. Additionally, high standards are sought by formal education that results in professional credentials. A graduate degree, usually a Ph.D. but sometimes a master's degree if that is the terminal degree (last of a course of study for a discipline), is a measure of the rigor of a researcher's training. Courses in methodology are usually included in a graduate program, and because most academic positions require active scholarship as a condition of tenure, academic professionals continue to stay current in research matters. The graduate degree is a credential by which the profession is able to set certain standards of scholarship. The profession seeks to establish benchmark standards for research by both these means, which helps all readers, regardless of status, to examine only the best results of the professions' research efforts.

One of the drawbacks to these methods is their tendency to favor those who are prominent members of the professional guild. Newcomers, particularly if they lack credentials, find it difficult to present their own findings, even if carefully prepared. Normally this is viewed as an acceptable trade-off, certainly among members of a profession with credentials, but occasionally there are valuable insights to be made outside the inner circle of prominent scholars. The main difficulty from the nonprofessional researcher's view is the evaluation of research done by members outside the professional guild. The educational background of the researcher is unknown, and the process of peer review is limited for amateurs. The seductive ease of self-publication on the Web, we have noted earlier, has tended to flood the world with information.

With respect to the design of most Internet search engines, the authority of the researcher responsible for the information is not generally a primary concern. If you are looking for material on linguistic syntax, a work by Noam Chomsky is no more likely to be retrieved than your next-door neighbor's home page on the Web if his files are well stocked with the keywords you entered for your search. A certain amount of skepticism is appropriate in examining Internet resources, particularly if the background of the author is unknown. This is especially true when one is dealing with emotional issues or opinion pieces, where evidence presented for a particular viewpoint is often equivocal at best.

Many of the characteristics of good quality mentioned in the section on evaluation of traditional research results hold true for Internet resources as well, perhaps even more so. In general, the origin of the information is the best first test. Although it is not always necessary to be suspicious, it never hurts to examine a researcher's motives and perspective critically. If not professional, what are the aims of the researcher? Do particular affiliations or agendas motivate the research? What perspective does the research seek to advance?

If you are satisfied with a worthy origin for the information, the next issue is the carefulness of the research itself. Is the evidence well presented? Are the arguments well supported — the documentation of the evidence solid and meticulous? Do the conclusions run counter to the accepted wisdom you have found in the rest of the professional literature? Do footnotes and bibliography indicate other resources? What other kinds of resources are suggested by the work? Are they all Internet resources as well, or does the author exhibit a solid grounding in a range of material?

Another clue to authenticity is the location of the information. Is it someone's Web home page? Is it sponsored by a university or other organization? Accountability is a part of authority, and because identity can sometimes be ambiguous (or deceptive) in an Internet environment, the origin of the information becomes highly significant for evaluative purposes. As mentioned earlier, logical consistency, as well as emotional tone, is also important.

Although it is often impossible to be perfect in this evaluation phase, your research will benefit from good attention to your resources. If you yourself are not skeptical of your resources, someone in your audience may be, and anticipating any objections and offering solid reasons why the information is valid, will strengthen your position considerably. These evaluative skills improve over time and are part and parcel of any good research effort.

Scholar's Workstation Model

One approach to research increasingly employed at the college level is known as the "scholar's workstation" model. This model involves a change in the process regarding the retrieval of information for scholarly inquiry. In this model, the scholar is equipped with a good personal computer and a reliable Internet connection. The scholar is able, through these technological innovations, to tap into information resources that are available online, store, organize and analyze the data in a way that is helpful to the study.

This idea is hardly a new one. As early as 1945 in a seminal journal article on technology and knowledge by Vannevar Bush ("As We May

Think," *Atlantic Monthly*) a grand idea of technological connection was proposed that would allow scholars access to information in a variety of formats in a unified interface. Although Bush, of necessity, talked about the latest technology of the day (microfilm), he clearly set the foundations for this model, and proved to be astonishingly prescient in the process. He went on to talk about the increasing saturation of information (in 1945!) and the difficulties of staying abreast of all that was relevant to one's interests. His horror at the current glut of information, since he died in 1974, can only be imagined.

The principal information point for this model involves access—an individual scholar's ability to reach the information resources needed for study. The traditional model utilized print-based tools—library catalogs, journal indexes, specialist bibliographies prepared by librarians or other researchers, letters of correspondence with other scholars, conference papers as well as the other facets of scholarly activity (face to face contact with other specialists, telephone contact, etc.). Depending on the discipline, there was often a fair amount of browsing that went on, either through books, back issues of journals in the library, or bibliographies created by other researchers.

The scholar's workstation model changes the nature of this access. The primary assumption is that "virtual access" is in most cases as good as actual physical access to the material in question. This assumption is more valid in some disciplines than others and obviously depends on the format of the material in question as well. For many primary resources, such as diaries, handwritten documents, medieval illuminated manuscripts, and the like, there is no substitute for bare-hands physical touch, for the document can provide enhanced levels of understanding (notes in margins, emotional flavor of the handwriting, etc.) impossible to convey digitally. On the other hand, if the material is truly rare and/or fragile, it may be available only to the upper echelons of researchers, and a digital copy to be disseminated will both preserve the original while offering a glimpse of its nature to a wider portion of humanity than otherwise might be possible.

In the "best case" scholar's workstation situation, the researcher is able to connect to valuable databases in his or her area of specialty, locate journal articles or other research publications written by scholars in the field, and read the information online. All this can be done from home or office—it is not necessary to actually be face to face with the material. Even if physical access to the material is still required (a book for example) the foraging stage of the research can often be done online. With access to the library catalog the right material can be identified, and then the scholar needs merely to visit the library with a list of call numbers to retrieve the material.

At the very least, some time is saved, and given the power and flexibility of modern library catalogs, often the search is more comprehensive and sophisticated than could have been achieved with a card catalog.

In the case of journals, the most complete scholar's workstation model has the journals in full-text format online, so that locating and reading an article is a seamless process. Full-text databases like Lexis-Nexis or Dow Jones Interactive permit fast online searches in their indexes for newspaper and other articles on a specific subject, and the desired full-text article is then just a mouse-click away from the researcher's avid and inquisitive mind.

Some of the traditional limitations of research are discarded in this model. Library collections can be searched from a hundred miles away, at any hour of the day or night. It is not necessary to trot one's way into the musty periodicals area of a university library to locate the latest articles on Baltic archaeology. Instead of having to read the material only in the library (many academic libraries do not permit journals to be checked out) or else to spend time and money photocopying the article, the scholar's workstation model permits the researcher to save the desired document by downloading, for digestion at whatever moment is deemed most desirable. The article can be printed out, for a physical folder of data, or saved digitally for reference later.

This independence from temporal and spatial limitations allows a "just in time" approach to data collection. Documents can be located and retrieved quickly, and in the best case, the range of the researcher may also be greater than in the traditional model. Multiple online journal indexes can be tapped, sometimes even with one broadcast search, in a way that was never possible with printed indexes.

This independence carries over to the manipulation of data in this model as well. The spreadsheet data from a science article on lemur distribution can be downloaded into the researcher's own spreadsheet software and manipulated. The citations from an online search can be saved for use in a bibliography or footnote for the scholar's own publication. Various bibliographic programs such as Endnote or Procite allow scholars to organize and format subject bibliographies for use in research activity.

Obviously this model places great stress on access, which varies from institution to institution. Typically wealthy so-called "Research I" institutions like the University of California, Yale, or MIT will have extensive, comprehensive indexes available for their scholars— students and faculty alike. Poorer institutions do not always have the same range or depth. But even here there are variations. Large public systems like the California State University system (CSU) or the State University system of New York

(SUNY) sometimes are able to wrangle extensive access to databases by virtue of their sheer size through consortial agreements. Access tends to be most problematic at poorer, non-affiliated institutions.

A potential drawback to this model is the tendency towards over-reliance on seductive new technology. While online access may increase the range and speed of discovery, it may not incorporate all the necessary information. Much of the world's best data is still found only in books, journals or other documents not available electronically in any way. The scholar often finds it necessary to continue to use the time-honored attributes of careful analysis. By paying close attention to the information uncovered, carefully examining the footnotes and other citation information from the best information uncovered, it may be possible to identify material that cannot be found electronically.

Another risk of this process is the tendency, particularly under time pressures, to grasp at the closest, most easily available electronic piece of data in neglect of more rigorous, fully developed information available only in traditional formats.

Another problem, one central to the mission of this book, is the necessity for technological training. The learning curve for some elements of the scholar's workstation model can be daunting, particularly if they extend beyond the fairly basic searching we have covered for library catalogs or databases. Statistical programs, data manipulation applications, and bibliographic utilities all take time to learn. Downloading certain types of data can prove to be an adventure at times, and network knowledge increasingly becomes helpful. Finding out ways to increase your knowledge and education in the right areas is important, and solutions are not always readily at hand.

Digitial files can provide their own difficulties too, in many ways that might be more amusing if they were less important. Anyone who has ever lost a file through carelessness or accident knows how frustrating it can be to rebuild such a file or rewrite an extensive document. One commonsense piece of advice, more elusive in practice that it should be, is to back up files religiously. Making copies of your bibliographies and searches, and duplicates of your data will hedge bets against the possibility of loss.

This raises some other issues regarding digital documents that call for some discussion. Digital documents (unlike printed words on good quality paper with a weather resistant hardcover binding) are notoriously fickle in their durability. Today's standards may be obsolete in five or ten years. How will you return to your sacred electronic files if you can no longer read them? At the moment, the best approach requires archival practices. Backup copies must be made regularly, often enough both to minimize physical degradation and technological obsolescence.

Another plus for the scholar's workstation model, however, is the opportunity to extend publication and dissemination of research findings. The Web has made online publication easy, perhaps too easy for some. But for scholars or anyone engaged in education, this has been mostly very helpful. Papers can be published online, as well as lecture notes for classes, syllabi, even grades at the end of the semester. While the requirements for most university faculty (and research specialists in any field) include publication of their work in peer reviewed journals, often the Web is a good place to put "think pieces" or second tier work. More and more online journals are peer reviewed, making an opportunity for scholars to publish their work more quickly and without some of the middle steps of publication (printing, subscription distribution through the mail, etc.) in traditional ways.

Of course a scholar's connection to the Internet also confers the capacity to communicate with other specialists as well. For many, this is the real boon of the Internet — the increased range and speed of scholarly communication.

While the scholar's workstation model is often imperfectly represented in practice, if added to the arsenal of a researcher's set of tools, it serves as a valuable extension of traditional research practice.

The Law and the Internet

The explosive growth of the Internet has caught legal and government institutions by surprise. Almost overnight, it seemed, we had in our hands a major communications network with hardly any specific laws governing its use. This has given the Internet a reputation for being an "anything-goes" environment. However, the legal professions and the governments of the world are catching up. There is a tremendous amount of debate about what and how laws should apply to the use of the Internet.

Even though the Internet may be one of the fastest evolving communications media we have ever known, it is by no means lawless. Many laws already in existence also apply to the Internet. In some cases the Internet may add a particularly interesting challenge to the enforcement of these laws. In yet other cases, governments around the world are racing to enact new legislation to govern an ever-changing technology — with varying levels of success. This chapter is not intended to provide specific legal advice. If you need legal advice concerning use of the Internet, contact a practicing attorney experienced in technology-, computer-, and Internet-related issues.

Common sense suggests that criminal activity is criminal activity whenever it occurs, and is defined by the rules of the society. The use of the Internet for or during the commission of a criminal act does not make the act any less criminal. Many of the legal issues surrounding the Internet concern the application of jurisdiction and enforcement. They will, over time, cause some changes in the laws governing the use of this new technology.

There are federal, state, and local laws governing the use of any communications medium: telephone, satellites, cable television, and so on. The Internet is an international network, so you may also need to consider international laws and the laws of other countries. The nature of Internet technology also adds an interesting twist to the defining of regulations and jurisdictions. If you send an email message from San Francisco to London, that message will travel in network lines across state lines and through other countries. In addition, due to packet switching, different segments of a single message may travel through different networks, states, and countries en route to the same destination. So the question may be asked: Whose law applies on the Internet? It could be argued that all jurisdictions apply on the Internet. However, in reality, this kind of governance can be very difficult to enforce due to the sheer size and scope of the Internet.

Acceptable Use Policies

Because the Internet grew out of federal research projects, the laws governing its use early on were under federal jurisdiction and were mainly restricted to actions directly related to the research project. It was not until 1995 that the National Science Foundation, which controlled the largest backbone on the Internet, relinquished its control to commercial telecommunications companies, thereby making the Internet a largely privatized venture. Still, no one "owns" the Internet. The Internet is composed of many networks owned and operated by many companies and organizations, each with its own rules or acceptable use policies (AUP).* These networks cross local, state, and national boundaries, even international waters, and can be broadcast from satellites orbiting the earth. Information on the networks is available to literally millions of potential users at any given time. Determining which rules govern your actions on the Internet can be a daunting task.

So how do you know what's right and wrong? First and foremost, the acceptable use policy of your ISP—whether it is your school, workplace, or a commercial provider—will determine what rules you must live by online.

*Not all ISPs refer to their guidelines as an "Acceptable Use Policy." Regardless, you are paying your ISP to provide a service—a connection to the Internet—and your acceptance of their guidelines statement or AUP is a condition of the service.

Each ISP has a set of rules that govern use of its services. Your ISP may have rules above and beyond any existing local, state, federal, or international laws. The following sample ISP from Best Internet Communications is typical:

> We have adopted a philosophy that assumes the honesty and good intent of our subscribers, therefore our services are provided in as unrestricted a manner as possible to allow our users to have the richest Internet experience possible.
>
> The extent of the "rules" that we enforce on our users is simply what the law demands of us.

Regulations

1. We are required by law to report any criminal activity that we become aware of. This applies particularly to software piracy. Be warned that if we find commercial software stored on our hard disk, we will report it and immediately terminate your service.

2. You may not make threats against another person via email or news or any other electronic media/service we provide. We are prepared to defend your right to free speech to our fullest ability, but we will not defend you if you violate this simple rule.

3. You may not mount an attack against our system or any other. This includes mail bombing (sending three or more unsolicited pieces of email or files exceeding 60K), "hacking" or attempting to gain root access, tsunami or flood bots or annoyance utilities like "nuke" or "flash."

4. You may not "spam" or flood the usenet with a single post to a large number of newsgroups not related to the topic of your article.

5. You may not "spam" people via email. This is defined as unsolicited (unwanted, unrequested) email sent to many people.

6. Forging of email or postings (to include cancel messages, whether manual or automated) will not be tolerated and will cause the offending account to be closed.

Our Rules

1. Only one dial-in per account at a time. This means that you cannot call in on two modems at the same time. You are allowed to Telnet in as many times at once as you like. If you are found logged in more than once over a modem connection we will automatically assume that your password has been compromised and will immediately suspend your account. There are some circumstances when we may permit multiple dial-ins, please contact us if you have a good reason to do so.

2. Trying to "hack" root login on our machines is forbidden.

3. Making public or providing any of our system files to other users of the Internet is forbidden.

4. It is forbidden to run packet sniffers or similar programs.

5. You may not disturb other users' files or directories.

6. You may not run software designed to cause our system to stop working correctly.

7. You may make whatever material you like available for FTP or WWW as long as it is legal. Users are given 200MB/day of bandwidth by default, and will be required to pay extra for any additional bandwidth they use. Please refer to the FAQ for specifics. For this reason, we do not recommend that users put adult material up for FTP/WWW, but we do not forbid it either.

8. We simply ask that our users use common sense and try not to do things that cause us or other users of our service or the Internet any real harm.

Best Internet Communications, Inc.
voice: (800) 764-2378   345 E. Middlefield Road
fax: (550) 940-6464   Mountain View, CA 94043
email: info@best.com   http://www.best.com

Please address comments about this page to webadmin@best.com.
© Copyright 1995-6 Best Internet Communications, Inc.

This AUP statement reflects the need of ISPs to place limits on the use of their resources so that they will be available for everyone. Internet resources are limited in the sense that hard disk space, transmission bandwidth, computer technology, and staff all require money and infrastructure. Abusing the system makes smooth and efficient operation difficult.

The AUP statements of ISPs usually reflect a combination of legal and ethical behavior guidelines and rules designed to provide equitable access and use of computing resources. As a condition of service (you normally have to agree to abide by the rules to gain access to the service), they are the first "laws" that govern your use of the Internet. Most ISPs include an "umbrella" statement about complying with all federal, state, and local laws, and they may state their willingness to cooperate with authorities in the enforcement of such laws.

Copyright and Intellectual Property

If you produce a document or any other creative work, you should be able to claim credit and or compensation for your efforts. Copyright and intellectual property laws protect your right to do so and protect you from anyone who tries to claim ownership or make profits from your work.

Copyright laws can vary from country to country. In the United States, copyright law is granted by the U.S. Copyright Act of 1976. The Internet was a research project in its infancy in 1976, but copyright laws still apply. Section 102 of the U.S. Copyright Act of 1976 states (emphasis added):

Copyright protection subsists, ... in original works of authorship fixed in any tangible medium of expression, *now known or later developed*, from which they can be perceived, reproduced, or otherwise communicated, *either directly or with the aid of a machine or device*. Works of authorship include the following categories:

(1) literary works;
(2) musical works, including any accompanying words;
(3) dramatic works, including any accompanying music;
(4) pantomimes and choreographic works;
(5) pictorial, graphic, and sculptural works;
(6) motion picture and other audiovisual works;
(7) sound recordings; and
(8) architectural works.

In other words, copyright extends to cover technologies that are as yet unknown, just as the Internet was relatively unknown in 1976. There is still a great amount of discussion about the Internet and its implications on copyright law. For the most part, all documents created on the Internet, including email, could be considered "literary works" and thereby protected by copyright. In addition, the Internet has multimedia capabilities — the ability to display and transmit text, graphics, video, and sound, which are also designated as "works of authorship."

Copyright protects the author of a work and grants him or her specific rights to its use. Section 106 of the U.S. Copyright Act of 1976 states [emphasis added]:

the owner of copyright under this title ... has the exclusive rights to do and to authorize any of the following:

(1) to *reproduce the copyrighted work* in copies or phonorecords;
(2) to *prepare derivative works* based upon the copyrighted work;
(3) to *distribute copies* or phonorecords of the copyrighted work to the public by sale or other transfer of ownership, or by rental, lease, or lending;
(4) in the case of literary, musical, dramatic, and choreographic works, pantomimes, and motion pictures and other audiovisual works, to perform the copyrighted work publicly; and
(5) in the case of literary, musical, dramatic, and choreographic works, pantomimes, and pictorial, graphic, or sculptural works, including the individual images of a motion picture or other audiovisual work, to display the copyrighted work publicly.

In other words, only the author or owner of the copyright of a work can give permission to use, copy, distribute, or display a copyrighted work. Copyright is obtained from the moment a work is created, whether a

© symbol is present or not. If a notice of copyright is given or present on a work, it should have a © symbol, the year of publication, and the name of the owner of the work. Copyright for works created on or after January 1, 1978, exist for the life of the author plus 50 years. Corporations or institutions may also obtain copyright, which lasts for 28 years from the original date of publication. In some cases copyright may be renewed and extended for an additional period.

Unauthorized use, copying, distributing, or displaying of another person's original work could be considered a violation of copyright. In addition, copying someone's work and denying the original author credit is a violation of copyright called plagiarism (see discussion below). If someone illegally uses a copyrighted work, such violation could be viewed as an infringement upon the copyright owner's ability to be compensated for her or his work. Although copyright is not designed solely to protect profits that can be gained from an original work, it is a fact that money is often made from copyrighted works. Violation of copyright can become a rather serious offense, especially when there is money or credit of authorship involved. Many lawsuits have been filed for violation of copyright, and the fines can be millions of dollars.

In 1994 the U.S. Department of Commerce's Information Infrastructure Task Force (IITF) Working Group on Intellectual Property Rights published a report entitled "Intellectual Property and the National Information Infrastructure." This report is still being debated, but it brings up some interesting issues with regard to new technologies and their effect on copyright law. With respect to new telecommunications technologies such as fax, satellite broadcasting, and the Internet, the report suggests adding "transmission" to the list of methods by which a copyright owner may distribute his or her work. When you consider all the documents and information available on the Internet, you begin to see how copyright affects the use of the Internet for research purposes. Files on the Internet, including documents, email, and even software programs, are transmitted from computer to computer, but there is still a significant amount of debate as to whether this amounts to copying or violation of copyright. Copyright law may need to be modified to reflect the influence of the Internet.

• *Fair Use of Copyrighted Materials.* It may begin to seem as if you cannot view, print, or use any information you find on the Internet without permission from the author. There are clearly some instances where formal permission should be requested (see discussion, page 47), but the Copyright Act of 1976 makes some exceptions for use of copyrighted material without expressed, written consent of the owner. There are special exceptions made for libraries, educational institutions, nonprofit displays or performances. The most widely known exception is referred to as "fair use."

Section 107 of the Copyright Act of 1976 states:

> the fair use of a copyrighted work, including such use by reproduction in copies or phonorecords or by any other means specified in that section, for purposes such as criticism, comment, news reporting, teaching (including multiple copies for classroom use), scholarship, or research, is not an infringement of copyright.
>
> In determining whether the use made of a work in any particular case is a fair use the factors to be considered shall include –
>
> 1. the purpose and character of the use, including whether such use is of a commercial nature or is for nonprofit educational purposes;
> 2. the nature of the copyrighted work;
> 3. the amount and substantiality of the portion used in relation to the copyrighted work as a whole; and
> 4. the effect of the use upon the potential market for or value of the copyrighted work.
>
> The fact that a work is unpublished shall not itself bar a finding of fair use if such finding is made upon consideration of all the above factors.

Although fair use rules seem to apply mainly to educational institutions and purposes, this does not give schools or training centers freedom from complying with copyright laws. Determination of whether an exception should be made for fair use of a copyrighted work is done on a case-by-case basis.

If you have an assignment to prepare a presentation on using the Internet to your fellow classmates or colleagues, you may be able to print a Web page and make copies for your class as an example. You may not, however, make a copy of this book and distribute it to your class. You also cannot sell copies of any copyrighted material to anyone without expressly granted permission from (and or compensation to) the copyright owner.

If you ever doubt whether your use of copyrighted material is considered fair use, you should seek permission from the copyright owner (see Seeking Permission to Use Copyrighted Material, page 50).

• *Public Domain.* When copyright expires, works enter the public domain, where permission is granted to freely distribute, copy, use, display, or perform a work. Generally speaking, a work is in the public domain if

1. Ownership of copyright has expired and was not renewed.
   Example: For some items published before 1978, owners failed

to renew their copyright when the original 28-year term expired. These items are now in the public domain.

2. Ownership of copyright has expired.
    Example: Materials published prior to 1923 have a copyright that lasts 28 years, with renewal in the 28th year extending the copyright to a total of 75 years. Materials published from 1923 to 1977, with renewal of copyright in the 28th year, are protected for a total of 95 years. For materials published in or after 1978, copyright will last for the life of the author plus 70 years. Hence, the full text of Louisa May Alcott's *Little Women* can be found on the Internet, copied, printed, and distributed, but the works of Stephen King are still copyrighted and are therefore not freely available or distributable.

3. Material is a federal government publication.
    Example: Publications such as the 1990 U.S. Census of Population and Housing, the full text of pending and active legislation, presidential speeches, the Declaration of Independence, the Constitution of the United States of America, and any other document published by the federal government are available on the Internet and are not copyrighted.

4. Owner grants permission for a work to be placed in the public domain.
    Example: The creator of a software program allows the program to be distributed freely, copied, and (in some cases) modified.

As with fair use, determining if a work is in the public domain may need to be done on a case-by-case basis. Again, if you are in doubt as to whether a work is in the public domain, you should seek permission from the original copyright owner.

• *Seeking Permission to Use Copyrighted Material.* If you are writing a report, preparing a presentation, or doing any other kind of research that requires you to use copyrighted material, you should seek permission from the owner of the copyright to use that material. The owner may grant permission, require a fee, or ignore your request altogether. Regardless, you should seek formal permission for use to ensure that your use is in compliance with the copyright laws.

Whenever possible, you should make this request for permission in writing.

There have been some legal cases recently where it is argued that permission is implied by the nature of the work and the actions of the owner.

Sample Permission Letter

[date]

[name and address of addressee]

Dear [name]:

I am writing to request permission to distribute the material specified below for [describe intended use in detail].

Material to be used: *[detailed description of material to be used and full citation of the original work]*

It is understood that full credit will be given to you and your company; please supply me with the credit and/or copyright notice(s) that should appear with this material.

Your prompt consideration of this request will be greatly appreciated. Please sign the release form below and return this copy of the letter to my attention at: [your contact information. Please make a copy for your files.

Thank you for your time and attention.

Sincerely,

[Your name and signature]

_____

I grant [your name] permission for the use requested above.

_____

Signature   Date

For example, it could be argued that email is a copyrighted work. If you receive an email message from someone and forward it to another person without the original sender's permission, you could be considered in violation of copyright. However, if you send a message to a mailing list where it is received by thousands of people and one person forwards it to another person, is that necessarily a violation of copyright or is it fair use? Did you forfeit your distribution rights by sending a message to 1,000 people in the first place? This is a very hotly debated topic, and the authors make no attempt to offer a solution or a guideline. Use of the Internet has already started great debates about existing copyright laws, and such debates will probably continue for many years to come.

• *Plagiarism.* Plagiarism is the act of stealing another person's work and taking credit for it yourself. It is a serious violation of both copyright law and societal ethics. Whenever you use the work of another person, you should always give credit to that person for the work he or she has done (see appendices). In cases where the original work is in the public domain, plagiarism is still punishable. In educational institutions, evidence of plagiarism may be punishable by denial of graduation or dismissal.

Plagiarism is not an invention of the Internet, but having access to information in electronic format makes it easier to incorporate that information into other documents, so the temptation to plagiarize can be greater. For instance, if you are doing a research paper on copyright laws, you can probably find a copy of the Copyright Act of 1976 on the Internet. Because it is in electronic format, it is easy to incorporate the information into your research paper — no need to go to the library, locate the printed edition, and type the information into your paper by hand. Simple. And the good thing is you are smart and have done your homework. You know that the Copyright Act of 1976 is a federal document, so it is not covered by copyright, and you will be sure to cite quoted sections.

Because it is easier, the temptation to copy someone else's work may be ever present on the Internet, but the ease with which it is done does not make it any less illegal or unethical.

Privacy Issues

Since you'll be using the Internet to do research, you need to understand some of the issues of being an Internet "citizen." One of those issues is maintaining your privacy and respecting the privacy of others. Once you log on to the Internet and use it to communicate with others, you are exposing yourself to every other person on the Net.

During your research you are bound to share in some discussions with other Internet users. It is wise to maintain your privacy when communicating on the Internet with people you don't know. There is a semi-illusion of anonymity on the Internet. Email addresses tell you very little about the people who use them: only the username (which may or may not be related to the person's real name) and the system on which she or he has an account. Usernames are sometimes referred to as handles, especially when they do not relate to the person's real name. Because of this anonymity, you have to learn to be cautious and use your own judgment when deciding whom to converse with and what information is truly reliable. In addition, it is wise to protect your own privacy by not revealing personal information such as home address, credit card numbers, social security number, or other identifying information unless you are absolutely sure that your privacy is protected. You should also respect others' privacy when it comes to email; do not forward messages without permission or send mail to those who have indicated that they do not want to receive it.

You also should be aware that information about *you* is probably floating around on the Internet somewhere. In the early years of the Internet, privacy was often taken for granted because there were no real tools to find people on the Internet. Today, however, there are telephone directories and workplace employee listings freely available online, many of them searchable by just having someone's real name or email address.

Ethical Issues and Censorship

In late 1995 Senator Jim Exon (R) brought the Telecommunications Act of 1996 to the floor of the Senate. Although the bill covered all telecommunications technologies and their use, Title V of that proposed bill was specifically aimed at regulating "broadcast obscenity and violence" and represented the first real attempt at regulating the content of the Internet. This bill is commonly referred to as the "Communications Decency Act" or CDA. The legislators endorsing the bill argued that some type of regulation was required to protect children from pornography on the Internet. The bill made it a criminal activity to make, create, solicit, or transmit "obscene ... or indecent" material. It also made service providers liable if such activities occurred on their service:

(a) Whoever –

(1) in interstate or foreign communications-

(A) by means of a telecommunications device knowingly-
(i) makes, creates, or solicits, and
(ii) initiates the transmission of, *any comment, request, suggestion, proposal, image, or other communication which is obscene, lewd, lascivious, filthy, or indecent, with intent to annoy, abuse, threaten, or harass another person*;

(B) by means of a telecommunications device knowingly-
(i) makes, creates, or solicits, and
(ii) initiates the transmission of, *any comment, request, suggestion, proposal, image, or other communication which is obscene or indecent, knowing that the recipient of the communication is under 18 years of age, regardless of whether the maker of such communication placed the call or initiated the communication;...*

(2) knowingly permits a telecommunications facility under his control to be used for any activity prohibited by paragraph (1) with the intent that it be used for such activity,

shall be fined under title 18, United States Code, or imprisoned not more than two years, or both; and...

(d) Whoever –

(1) in interstate or foreign communications knowingly-

(A) uses an interactive computer service to send to a specific person or persons under 18 years of age, or

(B) uses any interactive computer service to display in a manner available to a person under 18 years of age, *any comment, request, suggestion, proposal, image, or other communication that, in context, depicts or describes, in terms patently offensive as measured by contemporary community standards, sexual or excretory activities or organs, regardless of whether the user of such service placed the call or initiated the communication; or*

(2) knowingly permits any telecommunications facility under such person's control to be used for an activity prohibited by paragraph (1) with the intent that it be used for such activity,

shall be fined under title 18, United States Code, or imprisoned not more than two years, or both.

Violation of this law was punishable by fines and up to two years in prison. In addition, an ISP who allowed any user to violate this law was also liable for fines and possible imprisonment.

The bill was passed and signed into law on February 2, 1996. In June 1996 a Philadelphia court ruled the CDA to be unconstitutional, and in July a New York court ruled the same. As you can imagine, a great deal of controversy surrounds Internet regulation. Much of it, although thought provoking, is beyond the scope of this book. However, it is worth noting some of the issues raised when debating indecency, free speech, censorship, and the Internet:

• Who defines "indecency"?

• If "indecency" and "obscenity" are defined by community standards, and the community is an international network, whose standards apply? The U.S.? Australia? China? France?

• If an ISP is required to monitor its users' activities to ensure they are not in violation of a statute such as this one, what does that do to the privacy of a user's files?

First Amendment themes involving the right to free speech come into play extensively in the Internet community. The issues for the Internet parallel other arenas, and eventually the decision comes down to where one will draw a line separating free speech, which is protected by the U.S. Constitution, from speech that is hateful, harmful, dishonest, or obscene. It is wise to note the spirit of the amendment, which grants the right of free speech but includes a responsibility to use it thoughtfully and carefully.

Another aspect of the free-speech debate centers on what sort of forum or medium the Internet should be classified as. Broadcast media, such as radio and television, have generally been more tightly restricted than other sorts of communication because they can be transmitted so easily and are entirely democratic about which houses they enter. For instance, anyone can wander into a room where a television is broadcasting a program and unintentionally — or intentionally — view what is on TV. Because of this, regulations exist to protect children, for example, from stumbling across what might be considered indecent material. For the Internet, one argument is that it is not broadcast media because you only find what you intentionally seek. To see a file, you must virtually go to its Internet location, and the decision to do so is made by you alone. For example, potentially offensive material is not beamed into your computer; it arrives only if you have intentionally sought it. Thus, the argument goes, regulation should not be as strict as with broadcast media because you take greater responsibility for the process of retrieval.

The free-speech dialog will continue, as it has throughout American history, and the Internet will find a place in the court rulings regarding free speech. You will do well to remember the awesome power and privilege that free speech provides and to take care that your Internet communication and use reflect your own responsibility and ethical foundation.

3
Internet Tools

Internet Beginnings and Basics

The Internet began in the late 1960s as a research project to determine the feasibility of interconnecting different types of computers and computer networks, primarily those used for military research purposes, over long distances. These computers were very large centralized computers called mainframes, controlled by one or more keyboard- and display-only devices called terminals. Although these terminals had keyboards and monitors, they did not have any processing power; the mainframe was the computer and the terminals were only the displays. A computer network is simply two or more computers linked together by a communications line, such as telephone lines or other cables. This project was funded by the U.S. Department of Defense, Advanced Research Projects Agency (DARPA).

In the late 1960s and early 1970s computers were relatively rare, usually found only in large research centers or universities. Sharing the processing power of these computers was important to the researchers primarily because at that time the computers were not by any means portable. In fact, the computers usually took up an entire room. The earliest version of the Internet consisted of very few computers across the country, with each computer using a different hardware configuration and a different operating system software. Hardware is the physical casing and electronic equipment that makes up a computer; software refers to the programs written for that particular hardware configuration. A series of protocols, or standards, were developed that allowed the different types of computers to communicate with each other.

From the Department of Defense's perspective, one of the initial values of the Internet was that it could serve as a reliable means of communication during a national crisis. Like other defense technologies, it was designed with the knowledge that its security could and would be compromised. By anticipating the difficulties that damaged cabling or broken computers would cause, the designers developed pathways and methods of electronic communication that were of extraordinary durability and efficiency. The route that data might take between computers on the network could vary greatly, depending on network traffic or problems. Data, such as an email message, were divided into small packets, smaller pieces of the file, and sent over the network toward their final destination. When the packets reached their final destination, they were reassembled. Different packets of data could take different paths to the destination and it would not matter, for they would be automatically reassembled and rendered coherent once they reached their final destination. This method of data transfer is called "packet switching."

The telephone system provides a good example of how the Internet works. Your telephone is connected to your local telephone company's system. When you place a phone call to another state, your call is routed to the system of the local telephone company in that state or area. When you connect to the Internet, your computer is on a network similar to the systems of phones that are connected by telephone lines. When you send an email message to someone over the Internet, your message is sent through one or more other networks until it reaches the local network of the recipient. When you request a document from a computer on a remote network, the same process occurs: that document is sent through one or more other networks until it reaches your local network and then your own computer.

The earliest uses of the Internet could be divided into three applications: transferring files, exchanging electronic mail (email), and using a remote computer. The transfer and sharing of files allowed researchers at remote locations to share information by connecting to each others' computers and copying, or downloading, files to their own computers. The exchange of electronic mail allowed the researchers to communicate with each other in a more timely manner than any other method available. This was, of course, before the widespread use of telephone answering machines. The ability to share and use another computer at some remote location was helpful because powerful computers were relatively rare and very expensive.

In 1986 a combination of factors came together to bring about a fantastic growth in the use of the Internet. One of those factors was the creation of the National Science Foundation backbone (NSFnet), a network of five super-computing centers at U.S. universities that allowed for rapid expansion of Internet connections for universities and colleges. Other factors included the decreased cost of computing technology and the expansion of communication capacity by the telecommunications industry.

This growth continued until 1990, with the introduction of the Hyper-Text Transfer Protocol (HTTP) and the development of the World Wide

Web (WWW or Web). The HTTP standard for transmitting documents over the Internet can be read by a WWW browser, software specifically designed for the Web. This technology has developed into the most popular aspect of the Internet, allowing users to send and display text, graphics, sound, and even video over the network. Since January 1993, the number of hosts, or individually accessible computers, on the Internet has approximately doubled every year (see Table 3.1). In 1995 NSFnet reverted back to a research network and passed control of its communication networks over to private enterprises.

Table 3.1:
Number of Internet Hosts*

Year (Jan.)	Hosts
1995	5,846,000
1996	14,352,000
1997	21,819,000
1998	29,670,000
1999	43,230,000
2000	72,398,092

No one knows for certain how many people these numbers represent. There are different methods for counting, but the trend itself is quite obvious. Every host has at least one user and may have thousands. For example, a system such as NETCOM, a popular Internet service provider, may count as one host, but there may be, at any one time, thousands of NETCOM customers accessing the Internet through that single host. It is extremely difficult to determine an accurate estimate for the number of users.

Uses of the Internet

Perhaps the most important feature that differentiates the Internet from any other communication network is that any person with access to it can be both an information user and provider. Unlike, for example, a television network, where content is controlled by a very limited number of individuals, anyone with access to the Internet can publish information of any description; it literally takes only minutes to do so. Furthermore, this information is then immediately available to millions of people worldwide. What started as an experiment in connecting networks has become a major

*Hobbes' Internet Timeline, Robert H. Zakorn; 2000, available http://www.isoc.org/guest/zakon/Internet/History/HIT.html#Growth

communications medium and source of information for millions of people. This effectively unchecked flow of information is a major driving force behind the development of the Internet as a communications and research tool.

The Internet is many things to many people, millions of people in fact. What are they using it for? The most popular uses seem to be sending and receiving electronic mail (email), participating in discussions, downloading software, and accessing the resources of another computer.

Information sharing is communication, and it can be as simple as sending an email message to a friend. It can also be as widespread as a software company notifying all of its users of an upcoming software update, the publication of an earthquake preparation manual, the availability of the text of pending legislation, or heated group discussion about the value of four- or six-cylinder automobile engines. All of these things are done on the Internet on a daily, and even hourly, basis.

Resource sharing is the ability to use the power and storage space of another computer. From your computer you can connect to a telephone directory database and search for individuals' phone numbers. This is much more efficient than adding additional hard drives and memory to your own computer so that you can create a database of the millions of individuals who have phone numbers. You can also connect to a computer on the Internet and read the collected works of William Shakespeare, refer to the *Elements of Style* by Strunk and White, or search Bartlett's *Familiar Quotations*—also more efficient than storing these works on your own computer.

Equally as important as storage is processing power. A powerful computer is required to maintain and search a database of all the millions of Internet sites around the world. However, you only have to connect to that computer over the Internet and submit a search request. That computer will do the search and then send the results back to you.

Educational Development of the Internet

Late in the 1980s many in academia had begun to realize the enormous potential for the Internet to act as a tool to enhance education. Small or remotely located schools and colleges could share in the resources developed by larger universities and agencies. Information could be disseminated without great difficulty. Distance no longer operated as the obstacle to education that it once did. Many kinds of technological advances that were once only in the hands of researchers became available to millions of people.

Some of the benefits the Internet provides for education include:

- *Remote access to data*— Remote users can search through huge resources such as the literature database or a company directory.

- *Easy data transfer*— Files of all sorts— text documents, software, pictures— can be transmitted easily through the Internet.

- *Enhanced communication*— Email and the use of discussion groups broadened avenues of communication between teachers of all varieties, increasing problem-solving abilities and theoretical and practical dialog. Electronic journals simplified some of the problems inherent in traditional journal publishing.

- *Distance learning*— Classes can be conducted from a remote location, with tests, homework, research papers, etc. all delivered electronically.

- *Research and development*— Many disciplines play a large part in the development, use, and distribution of Internet technologies.

One of the challenges presented by Internet technology is how the educational opportunities of the Internet can be made available to everyone. It takes relatively little reflection to note that although the Internet is "free" in the sense of what is available, it has plenty of "hidden" and "not-so-hidden" costs. Computer equipment, software, Internet service providers, telephone, and network wiring all cost money. Many colleges and universities are involved in the development of Internet technology and have the infrastructure to support it. However, this infrastructure is not "free." Besides wiring within buildings, economic issues are connected with finding usable personal computers and well-trained staff to oversee and operate them. Despite this, there are many who are trying to deliver access to the Internet to everyone. For instance, in March 1996 volunteers gathered across the United States for NetDay 96 to begin an ongoing effort to install fast network connections to schools across the country. Once this cabling infrastructure is in place, Internet education in schools will be available to children who would not normally have access to this kind of technology.

Commercial Development of the Internet

Although the genesis of the Internet was motivated by military research, its primary growth in the 1980s had been in education, particularly at the university level. The same kinds of things that work well for education (quick, inexpensive dissemination of information, ability to reach thousands of people by simple means, exchange of all kinds of data) also serve commercial interests extremely well. Recognition of this fact led to an explosion of commercial development on the Internet in the late 1980s that continues to this day.

Early commercial uses of the Internet included the exchange of electronic mail with subscribers of online services such as MCI Mail and CompuServe. In 1990 the first commercial Internet service provider, The World (http://world.std.com/), went online. Much of the early corporate presence on the Internet was either computer related or simple, billboard-like advertising for a limited number of products or services. Since the introduction of the World Wide Web, a graphical user interface to the Internet, commercial enterprises have been the fastest growing segment of the Internet.

Since 1995 the growth of businesses on the Internet has exploded to include not only advertising but product and service information, public relations, shopping, and much more. Marketing departments take notice of the 250 million or more Internet users who can be considered potential customers. Inherent in the commercial use of the Internet are the economic benefits to be derived from all involved, from jobs to purchasing merchandise. In addition, a business of one employee can have as much of a presence on the Internet as a corporation with thousands of employees. Anyone with a message to spread or a product to sell can make her or his presence known on the Internet. The limits to the commercial use of the Internet are unimaginable.

Applications and Implications in Research

Ironically, this cold war invention has developed into one of the largest international communications tools ever known. Unlike television or radio, the Internet is a two-way communications link. Average individuals cannot afford to create their own television or radio stations to discuss and share their interests, but they can create an Internet presence through email and the WWW. The Internet provides the fastest and most extensive method to share information with millions of people. This function alone has a great impact on the way individuals conduct research.

Here are some real-life research examples:

• A student needed to know the date of the wreck of the *Edmund Fitzgerald*, a freighter ship that sank in Lake Superior in 1975. Surprisingly, the information was not available in the *1995 World Almanac* listing of famous shipwrecks, but a quick search of the Internet led to the WWW home page of the SS *Edmund Fitzgerald* Bell Restoration Project at Michigan State University. This page not only included the date of the wreck but other detailed information concerning the ship, cargo, personnel, and the factors contributing to the sinking of the SS *Edmund Fitzgerald.*

- A small-business owner needed a copy of a nondisclosure agreement (NDA). An archive of business-related legal documents was located on the Internet; included among them was a sample NDA.
- A voter wanted to see the complete text, not just a summary, of a local ballot measure before he made his decision about voting on it. He was able to find it on his municipality's WWW site.
- A laboratory technician working with infectious organisms needed more information about the use of a new design in lab suits and through email and discussion groups was able to survey and interview lab workers from around the world.
- A parent felt that he needed to know more about a movie that his children wanted to see. Using Yahoo!, an Internet search service, he was able to find multiple movie-related WWW sites. From these many sites, he was able to get reviews, both from professional movie critics and from dozens of moviegoers.
- An investor wanted to see the latest financial reports of the companies she had invested in. She was able to find the actual Securities and Exchange Commission (SEC) filings for each one of these companies.
- A potential buyer wanted to research new automobiles and compare the features of each model. She was able to find both manufacturer's and independent data and reviews, as well as comments from current owners of the same model cars. Using this information, she was able to evaluate each model's features and options without the high-pressure experience of visiting an automobile showroom.

Traditionally, when conducting research for personal, professional, or educational purposes, you needed to go to some type of research center or refer to a printed source of information. Often, research required going to a library and using catalogs, directories, indexes, and other materials. Many of these types of resources had been computerized but were often limited to on-site use. However, with the advances in computer technology and the widespread use of the Internet, on-site use might not always be necessary. In addition, traditional research often required using information published through some type of professional publishing process: magazines, journals, newspaper articles, or books. On the Internet anyone can publish information covering any subject area. As we have seen, this can be both a blessing and a curse in conducting research on the Internet. Not only will you find more extensive information than you would find among printed resources, but you will also find resources that exhibit no "editorial" or other quality control over the information provided.

The Internet as a Community

The Internet has always welcomed new researchers, and now, sometimes grudgingly, it accepts the rest of the population, whose interests are not always those of the academic or research community. We will examine more fully some of the aspects of community ethics on the Internet (or "netiquette" as it is often termed) later in this chapter, but it is worth remembering that civil discourse and consideration for others is as important in online communities as in any other. A mature, nonthreatening attitude expressed in one's research questions and Internet communication maximizes the opportunities for productive dialog on the Internet.

Electronic Mail

Email is one of the fabulous windfall profits of Internet development. It remains the most commonly used of all the Internet applications, and it has become a ubiquitous part of modern corporate and academic life. We have mentioned the ease, speed, and range of email and how it has transformed communication in contemporary society. Its benign qualities are legion and its drawbacks few.

Email can exist apart from the Internet. There are interoffice email systems that operate on a LAN (Local Area Network) and do not connect to the Internet. Typically in these systems you could send messages to any other people with computers on the network, and in turn you could receive messages from anyone connected to the local network. Some of these systems are quite sophisticated, making it easy to send mail, forward messages on to large groups of people, attach files and other nontext documents to messages, and even have assorted fancy features like the ability to set a specific time to send a delayed message. In the recent past these systems tended to be extremely powerful and user friendly but could not always extend their features when connecting to the Internet beyond, if they even were capable of reaching it at all. Internet mailers tended to possess opposite characteristics. They were not always simple to use, and although many powerful functions were available (such as sending attached files), the methods of accomplishing those features were not always easy or intuitive. UNIX operating systems had a few different varieties of simple mailers, while VAX systems had rugged but cumbersome systems.

Various front-end packages were developed to make email easier to use; among the earliest were "pine" (Program for Internet News and Email) and "elm" (for electronic mail), still used by many systems as alternatives to the simple UNIX Mail. Choice of mailing system is sometimes dependent on your ISP and how your own account is set up. Differences between mailing systems are roughly equivalent to the differences between word processing programs, although perhaps less marked. There are usually a half-dozen commands that one needs to memorize to make mailing easy, with another dozen or two that expedite more advanced or complicated functions. As usual, a lack of standardization is a common complaint, and in fact there is no good reason for the variety of commands used in the different systems.

Common mailers used at present include Eudora and Microsoft's Outlooker mailer, which work equally well on large accounts such as are found at universities and corporate networks, as well as small local networks. There are also increasingly hosts such as Yahoo! and Hotmail who provide free Web-based mailsystems. As usual, "free" must be properly understood — often this means that an advertising banner from the host is included in every email you send.

A drawback to Eudora, and various other proprietary systems, is that often the default settings limit mail to the machine that you are using. Messages stay resident with the machine, unless copied to floppy disk, in which case they become as portable as any other data. Many of us who are likely to use a range of computers during the day (from Macintoshes to PCs to Unix-based machines) like the flexibility that comes from not using a resident system like Eudora, and we like to be able to access mail from any platform.

Various commercial service providers offer their own mailing systems as well, generally making communication extremely convenient to others sharing the same provider, but sometimes posing complications with other Internet correspondents. An old joke of early email involved the differences between LAN mail and Internet mail. For the former, it was extremely easy to send mail to an extremely small number of people. For the latter, you could reach the whole world, but sending even the simplest message was neither easy nor intuitive. The two have grown closer together, to the benefit of most of the user community.

It does not really matter what mailing system one uses, as long as the basic operation is mastered. With email, you can do the following things:

• Send a message to anyone connected to the Internet

• Receive a message from anyone connected to the Internet

• Send information to multitudes of people

• Forward messages and files to others

- Participate in mailing lists to follow your research interests
- Subscribe to electronic journals

Email Operation

For Internet email, as opposed to LAN mail, the first requirement is an address. Without an address, email cannot function. Messages must be generated from a particular location on the Internet and must be received at a particular location. To use email you must activate your mailing system, which then allows you to view a list of incoming messages, which you can browse to select messages to view on your screen. Sending a message requires activating what is often called the "compose" function, where you may type the body of your message, adding an address to the email "envelope" and then issuing the command to send the message on to its recipient.

Except for the most primitive systems, which may be your own situation if you are using a UNIX or VMS platform, most of the commands tend to be fairly obviously arranged, and good mailing systems have menus or cues for the various commands and do not require you to practice unusual amounts of memorization. If you do have only a basic UNIX, VMS, or some other mailer, however, you may want to refer to a guidebook or manual for the specific methods of use.

The commonly supported features of most mailing systems include the following: sending and receiving standard email, forwarding on to others a message you have received, creating an address book of frequent correspondents and their addresses or "aliases" (great help for the memory), and putting received mail into folders or special locations. A variety of other special features may also be available, depending on the system you are using.

It is important to realize a bit of what goes on in email, and the new easy-to-use mailing systems make it appear a seamless operation, although many operations are going on in the background. Originally there was only one mail protocol, SMTP (Simple Mail Transfer Protocol), that operated on the Internet, and it seems awkward and archaic now. Shortcuts were few or depended on a fairly sophisticated knowledge of the operating system on which it was lodged. The current standard with the greatest usage is MIME (for Multi-purpose Internet Mail Extensions), which allows greater flexibility with mail and an ability to send nontext files as well as regular mail. Although the Internet is often criticized for a lack of standards, there are groups that work very hard to make usable standards for protocols and Internet applications. Although the centrifugal tendencies of individualism (and increasingly profit) may limit adoption of such standards, their overall utility is recognized by most Internet citizens, and progress continues toward more widespread use of accepted standards.

Email systems always include some sort of text editor that allows you to type a message and include basic kinds of text information. They tend to be rather primitive, without any of the formatting and other handy features that most word processors now incorporate, but they enable you to create a document and send it.

Receiving a message often involves invoking the text editor to view the message sent to your mailbox. When forwarding a message to someone else, or replying to the sender of the message, you usually are given the capacity to use the text editor again to crop or alter the message, perhaps including commentary or parenthetical notes. When replying to a message, the email system automatically notes the origin of the message and copies it to the "send to" part of the address for a reply.

An email message contains more information than is usually visible to you on your own screen. Messages come with "headers" that include information about where the message came from, with date and time notes, protocol used for sending, etc. Most of the time having this information displayed is of no interest to the receiver (and may also be system dependent and unalterable), so it is usually hidden. Occasionally, when experiencing email troubles, it is useful to see the header information in an attempt to diagnose what is going wrong. The mailing system will use this information as part of its normal function, as when replying to a message sent. The address is part of the header, and the system plucks the address of origin and applies it to the new outgoing "envelope" at the same time that it appends your own address to the envelope as the "return address." Here is a sample of an email header with date and origin information:

```
From rhoffman@sfsu.edu Sun Sep 15 09:45:28 1996
Date: Fri, 12 Apr 1996 15:28:58 -0700 (PDT)
From: Richard Hoffman <rhoffman@sfsu.edu>
To: NED LEE FIELDEN <fielden@sfsu.edu>
Cc: "DEBBIE C. MASTERS" <dmasters@sfsu.edu>
Subject: Library Lecture
```

When a message is "bounced" back, much of this header information is made visible, and as the sender you are able to view the attempted transaction. The information can often be deciphered, and the most common reason for a bounce is a bad address, resulting from a mistyped username or domain name. Other less-common reasons for a bounce can include problems related to network traffic or the sending or receiving systems.

Although initially email was designed purely for text, the capacity to include nontext information has improved over time. With many systems one can send all kinds of files along with a message by using attachments that append the file to the message. Newer protocols such as MIME allow nontext files to be transmitted, which is often handy for sharing documents created in a word-processing or other special application. Although one may think of a document created in a word processor such as Word as a "text-based document," in fact it is a binary file. Many word-processing codes are embedded in the document, which keeps it from being a "plain vanilla" text file.

Research Value of Email

All the features of email are really just facets of communication. The value for research interests is in the way that email may be used to further understand and bridge gaps in knowledge. This may be accomplished in several ways:

- Subscriptions to discussion groups
- Contacting authorities in the area of your interest
- Conducting interactive research

Discussion groups are covered in the next session, but they are based on email protocols and are worth a mention here. Mail from discussion groups comes to your mailbox just like any other mail. You may send mail to discussion groups, which are organized along the common interests of the members. Thus, if your research interests lie in the area of anthropology, by subscribing to an anthropology discussion group, you are able to participate in a dialog about anthropological issues. You read mail from the discussion group and are able to send questions or other ideas to the rest of the group. This is one way that email allows you to reach a wide range of individuals with interests similar to yours.

Authorities in the area of your interest can assume many different guises. Sometimes they are professionals at the upper levels of research; sometimes they are colleagues in your office or educational institution; sometimes they are friends at a distance or just informed people from around the world. When you need to know something, or are at a loss as to where to turn for ideas for the right resources, it helps tremendously to put the questions to the people best able to answer or direct you. In the past there were often obstacles to this very natural desire. Although researchers in a given area may be clustered in a small area or region of the world, usually they are spread all over the world. Even if they are concentrated in one area, that may not be in your own backyard. To meet, talk, or correspond with them used to take some effort, and often it was necessary to rack up a large phone bill, travel to expensive conferences, or engage in written correspondence that tended to involve fairly lengthy time delays in the exchange of information. Although all of these methods have their own value and should by no means be neglected by those serious about their research interest, email presents some intriguing solutions to some of the shortcomings of these methods.

Email Cost

Email is often a free benefit, depending on your work or educational institution. Computer accounts have become fairly common perks at universities and colleges and are often a part of many employment situations. Even if that is not the case, a computer account from a commercial ISP generally has a fairly nominal fee, usually not wildly different from a basic phone charge of $20 or so a month. The difference from a phone bill and email lies in the way the charges are structured. Many computer accounts have no limits on volume of mail and certainly no restrictions on distance. Email sent to Australia from New York has no user cost difference from email sent across town. Additionally, there are no extra costs for email sent to a large number of people at the same time.

Although email has some drawbacks in nuance compared to a face-to-face conversation at a conference or similar situation, it also has some advantages. Email, unlike a phone call or a chance encounter in a conference room, is a wonderful boon for the busy or distracted recipient. An email with questions can be dealt with when one has a chance to think clearly. Phones and personal encounters, while contributing positively to research in their immediacy and possible serendipity, do not always produce well-thought-out responses because they are capable of engaging others when they are preoccupied with other business. Email, on the other hand, can be answered immediately, if appropriate and possible, or at leisure, when time or resources permit. If questions require looking up information, that can happen on the recipient's time line and at his or her convenience. This often results in better transmission of accurate information and sometimes eliminates excessive relays of voice mail or other contacts.

In particular, email can be an excellent way to plan meetings and arrange schedules. It can reach a number of recipients quickly and remains somewhat between the permanence of a written record and the fluidity of a phone message. Unlike the somewhat cumbersome distribution lists possible in voice mail systems, most email systems allow you to make a distribution list fairly easily, and sending messages to several people is no more difficult or time consuming than to one.

Time

Email is fast. It does not require that the receiver be free at that time, as in phone systems. Unlike postal mail or "snail mail," email can be exchanged quickly. Usually the reply message takes a fraction of the time of regular mail and depends solely on the recipients' access to their email computer and their ability to answer the mail sent. For around-the-world communication, it can be especially valuable. Companies in California with offices abroad often make use of this speed. Questions for overseas personnel working on the same project can be sent in the evening of one day and arrive almost instantaneously at the mailbox of the recipients, who can then reply the next morning. Turnaround time can be very short and of course does not involve phone costs or other drawbacks.

Attachments and Viruses

The increasing ability of email to handle "attached files" or "attachments" means that a great deal of material, binary files that can include photos, graphs, and word processed documents, that previously was difficult to transmit by email is now effortless. This ease and flexibility has come with a cost however, as many users discovered in March 1999 with the spread of the Melissa virus. This virus tagged along as an attachment to email sent out to an astonishingly wide range of the Internet community. It damaged files and caused all sort of trouble to a number of people. Plain text email is just words, and cannot damage any files or computers, but attachments can carry executable files, that in Melissa's case were macros that replicated and spread to other files. It turned out that many mailers had minimal security, and the ILOVEYOU virus a year later (both are technically "worms") took addresses from the individual's addressbook and sent mail to unsuspecting friends, thus spreading by replication in a pattern all too familiar to biological diseases. In general, it is best to regard attached files from those you do not know with some suspicion, and at the very least be prepared to run virus protection software before opening new files. With the ILOVEYOU virus, even the protection of personal friendship was insufficient, since the virus spread among "friends."

Research Opportunities

Email also offers an opportunity for data gathering. If your research involves an interview, survey, or questionnaire, email can often serve as a valuable means for distribution. The value for your research depends a lot on the nature of the information you need to gather. Some interviews need a very high degree of interaction, which can only be accomplished in a face to-face or phone encounter. On the other hand, if for your methods it is important to ask identical questions to all participants, email can make for a standardized form, which is sent to all respondents. Respondents can read the survey and oftentimes respond more completely or thoughtfully than if questioned by phone or in person.

Sometimes a discussion group can form a potential forum for research gathering, and questionnaires can be sent to the entire group. You may have to be careful on this front, however, as noted in the section on discussion groups, because not all groups appreciate mass mailings.

Email is sometimes an option for saving bibliographic records as well. Good online library catalogs, such as the University of California's Melvyl catalog, will allow the results of a search to be emailed to the remote user, thus creating a way to document potential resources. This can be saved in a file for future reference.

Here is a sample of an email sent from a library catalog (UC's Melvyl system melvyl.ucop.edu) with a bibliographic record:

> From MELVYL@uccmvsa.ucop.edu Sat Jul 19 11:31:38 1997
> Date: Fri, 18 Jul 97 11:43:39 PDT
> From: Melvyl System <MELVYL@uccmvsa.ucop.edu>
> To: fielden@info.SIMS.Berkeley.EDU
> Subject: (id: FFX31651) MELVYL system mail result
> Search request: F SU INTERNET AND DATE 1997
> Search result: 98 records in the TEN-YEAR Catalog database
>
> Display: 20,32,34,41,56,75 TAGS
> 20.
> AN   3281203
> DB   Ten Year
> DT   BOOK
> PA   Trinkle, Dennis A.,
> MT   The history highway : a guide to Internet resources
> PL   Armonk, N.Y.
> PU   M.E. Sharpe
> DP   1997
> PG   xii, 249 p.
> DE   24 cm
> LO   UCD Shields D16.255.C65 H58 1997 Hum/SS Ref
> LO   UCI Main Lib D16.255.C65 H58 1997 Reference
> LO   UCSB Main Lib D16.255.C65 H58 1997
> LO   UCSD Undergrad D16.255.C65 H58 1997
> ZZ

Discussion Groups

A discussion group is a forum on the Internet where people can discuss issues and interests that they have in common. These groups are a driving force on the Internet, both in the development and use of its technology and in the forming of its culture. However, discussion groups are not only technology related. The entire spectrum of personal and professional interests and expression are represented in these groups. The topics that are represented cannot possibly be described in a simple sentence because, as of last count, there were over 20,000 unique discussion groups available, and the number changes *daily*.

Discussion groups are not interactive; they do not allow for online, real-time conversation. However, by using email, a slightly delayed form of a group conversation can take place with users sending email back and forth to each other and the group. You send an email message to a discussion group that is read by many people and they may choose to reply to your message, thereby furthering the discussion.

Advantages to Research

Discussion groups can be a major resource in research due to the fact that they can put you in touch with other people who are interested in the same topics that you are researching. You can use discussion groups as a forum to pose a question or problem. There is no guarantee that anyone will reply to you, but odds are good that they will, especially if your posting is a well-thought-out, well-constructed message.

You could also become a "lurker," someone who simply eavesdrops in on the conversation to gain a better understanding of a topic. Subscribing to a mailing list does not require that you post messages or replies; it is a voluntary system. Sometimes reading what other people have to say is the best way to gain a better understanding about something.

Using Discussion Groups

There are basically two kinds of discussion groups on the Internet: mailing lists and newsgroups. The differences between the two types are in the method of access to the discussion. Mailing lists are similar to postal mailing lists in that a single piece of mail is copied to multiple recipients. Messages posted to the mailing list are sent to the incoming mailboxes of all recipients on that list, so access to email is the only requirement to participate in a mailing list. With newsgroups, individuals send mail to a news server, which is a computer that maintains all the mail in a central location. In general, accessing newsgroups requires access to a news server provided by your ISP and a newsreader application, a client application that interacts with the news server to read newsgroup postings.

The number of postings, or messages, to a discussion group can vary greatly, depending on the subject of the group. Some groups or lists are devoted to informing users of certain products, and they may have relatively few postings per year. Other groups and lists are devoted to subjects that invite a more free-flowing conversation and can have over a hundred postings per day.

Some Internet discussion groups are moderated or monitored by an individual or individuals responsible for maintaining subject "integrity." This is to make sure that the discussion taking place stays within the subject matter of the group and helps to keep the volume of mail down to a manageable volume. It is very easy to get distracted in a slightly delayed conversation, allowing for topics such as operating system preferences to take over a discussion group devoted to using the Internet to teach classes. Many groups, however, are unmoderated. This can be both a blessing and a curse. It is a blessing because it allows for free expression and discourse of ideas, allowing anyone to join in and any opinion to be heard. It is a curse because there is often no way to easily separate out the "junk mail" from the true discussion. Junk mail in a group can be anything from an unrelated subject to an advertisement. It is considered a breach of netiquette to post an unrelated message to a group, but it often happens, either by mistake or ignorance.

When you post a message to a list or newsgroup, be sure to include a short subject description of your message. This helps other readers identify your message and allows them to decide whether they want to read it. This is especially important for mailing lists because your posting will go into someone else's incoming mailbox, thereby taking up disk storage space. If you reply to someone else's message, be sure that your reply includes the same subject. This assists readers in identifying related postings, or threads, in a list or group.

Members and participants tend to have a great deal of control over the tone and behavior of the discussion. To keep things civil, there are a few netiquette pointers you should always follow:

• When submitting a post, define your subject and post to related lists or groups only.

• When asking for information or assistance, be very clear about your request, providing as much information as possible.

- Use proper grammar, spelling, and tone. Be very careful about sarcasm, jokes, or other types of speech that may be misinterpreted.

- Do not "flame" or send aggressive messages (see end of chapter on Internet Culture, page 96).

All the usual suggestions regarding netiquette apply here, even more strongly than we have worded earlier. Your messages are being read by a large number of people (potentially thousands). Newcomer mistakes are usually tolerated, although rude people will pounce on you regardless of the innocence of your post. Often there are a handful of obvious questions a new subscriber might be tempted to ask. A week or two of lurking might answer them without the need for a message to the group. Many lists and groups are well mannered and welcoming to new members, but it is helpful to remember that you have just joined a new community, and some deference and discretion on your part will speed and smooth your entry to that community.

Many mailing lists are duplicated as newsgroups and vice versa. There are pros and cons to both, but it basically comes down to the type of access you have and your personal preference. Many also have FAQ files, a list of frequently asked questions, that explain their scope and purpose and any details that might help a new subscriber.

• *Mailing Lists.* Mailing lists have a huge range of topics and participants. There are mailing lists devoted to medieval history, Buddhism, computers in education, anthropology, creative writing, geology, announcements of new software releases, and a host of other subjects. Their range of style and interest level vary enormously as well. The tone of the discussion may be formal or informal, but all serve as a forum for their members to voice opinions and share ideas.

The first step in participating in a mailing list is finding one that interests you. There are thousands of lists available, so finding one that matches your interests is generally not difficult. You may be referred to a mailing list by a friend or colleague. In other cases you may see mention of a particular list in your readings or email. There are many "lists of lists" maintained and available on the Internet. Some of these references are mentioned in Chapter 5 of this book, but for now we will start with an example:

```
List Name: COMHIST
Description: History of human communication
Server: listserv@vm.its.rpi.edu
Instructions for subscribing:
Send email to: listserv@vm.its.rpi.edu
```

with the following message:
subscribe COMHIST <first_name> <last_name>

Mailing list subscriptions and the distribution of messages are primarily handled by server software. In other words, there is not another person receiving subscription requests and adding your request to the mailing list; a computer is handling your request to join the list. Therefore, any instructions you receive for subscribing to mailing lists must be followed *exactly* as stated.

Soon after you send your email subscription request, it should be confirmed by the server software. Depending on the type of list, you may also get an email message with instructions for using and maintaining your subscription. You will also be notified of the distribution address of the list. This email address is *different from the subscription address.* This can be a source of confusion for the new user. The subscription address is used to sign on to or off of a list or otherwise change the way your mail is handled. The distribution address is the address to use when sending a message to the list to be distributed to all the other members. You need to keep track of both of these addresses.

Examples of mailing list server software include Listserv, Listproc, Majordomo, Mailbase, and Mailserv. Listserv is used on the BITNET network (one of the many networks that make up the Internet), Listproc is used on UNIX-based servers, and Mailbase is mostly used on European networks. With different software come different commands and instructions. However, the server software should notify you by email if there is a problem with your message and give instructions to help you diagnose what went wrong.

Once subscribed, you will receive email from the list from all the members who have contributed messages to the list since the time that you joined. You will notice that all the mail comes from the distribution address of the list, not the subscription address. You can send notes or questions to the distribution address, which then automatically will get sent on to all the other members of the list.

Advantages and Disadvantages to Using Mailing Lists. In practice mailing lists offer two advantages for a given research interest. The first is the ability to stay in touch with a group of individuals with similar interests, who can exchange questions, comments, or whatever material is deemed of interest to the group. The exchange happens as quickly as email operates so that discussion can take place at a relatively quick pace. And because the mail arrives in your mailbox, you can deal with it whenever you find it most convenient. The members of the list form a type of community, and there are wide differences among mailing list communities in the way that they deal with issues, disputes, disruptive behavior, and various other crises. The collective behavior (and overall usefulness) of the lists, like so much else we will observe on the Internet, mirrors the humans who constitute them. A well-informed, civil, thought-provoking mailing list is a delight and is capable of furthering one's research interests considerably. An ill-mannered, argumentative mailing list can be infuriating, full of expressions of immature petulance and a lack of good information, but in the great democratic tradition, mailing lists will continue to exist as long as there is interest enough (and a base of subscribers) to keep them going.

The other area of particular utility in a mailing list is that it is possible to get a very quick and accurate answer to a specific question from those who know the subject area well. On many academic areas of interest, a frequent request is made for what kinds of further study is necessary for a given topic. For example:

> Dear Historians,
>
> I am interested in the economic development of the Punjab region in India during the time period from 1600 to 1800. In particular, I am interested in trade routes and kinds of crops grown there. I have read Mallory's _Central Asian Trade with India_ and Ferguson's _Pre-Modern Economic Development in Northern India_. Does anyone have any other suggestions for further reading? Why isn't there more contact with China at this time?
>
> Many thanks,
> Ned Fielden
>   San Francisco State University Library
>   fielden@sfsu.edu

This message includes a brief but appropriate inquiry and gives the kind of background information that might assist someone in making a good response (i.e., what I have read already). It also provides an email address at the end as a courtesy, and an affiliation, which often helps the respondent to know something about the nature of the writer's work or interest. With any luck, someone will respond with a suggestion for further reading, directing the writer to other works or perhaps cautioning him against taking Mallory's work too literally.

When posting a message to a mailing list, keep in mind that it will be going into the incoming mailboxes of all the subscribers on the list. They will have to act upon it in some manner: read, reply, or delete. Do not send "frivolous" or flame-filled messages to the entire list. Becoming the target of a large group of people's collective aggravation does not make for a pleasant experience on the Internet.

The list does not, and should not, function as a substitute for further research, but combined with it allows you to stay in touch with other people who share your interests.

The primary disadvantage of using a mailing list is the volume of mail it can generate, adding to the mail you may already be receiving from other sources. This, however, depends on your mail setup. If you are using a client application on your own computer to read your mail, then the amount of storage space it uses is up to you. If, however, you use a mail application like pine or elm to read your mail on your ISP's server, there may be limits to the amount of space your ISP gives you for storing your mail. Many mailing lists are moderated and frivolous postings are weeded out, so this may not become a problem for you.

• *Newsgroups.* Newsgroups are one of the oldest developments in Internet popular culture. Although similar in purpose to mailing lists, they present a different method of information dissemination. The difference is akin to the way information may be disbursed at your office. Some mail gets delivered right to your door or mail basket, but other information is posted at the main bulletin board in the lobby. For mailing lists, you stay "home" and the mail comes to you. For newsgroups, you must use the newsreader software to go to the news server and read the messages posted there.

The range of topics offered by newsgroups is truly astonishing. There are over 18,000 newsgroups available at this writing, and new ones are created every day. They represent the Internet in one of its most outlandish, chaotic, democratic, uncensored, outspoken aspects. There are many wonderful groups that serve as support groups for a myriad of topics and all sorts of helpful forums to deal with questions of many varieties. Newsgroups tend to be less formal than mailing lists, both in the range of topics discussed and in the tone of the discussion. Newsgroups are also referred to as USENET or USENET news. The USENET was one of the early networks that, along with NSFnet and BITNET, constituted the Internet. The USENET was designed to carry these newsgroups.

Messages posted to a newsgroup do not come from a community of subscribers such as the mailing lists, so the issues of accountability and responsibility are more problematic. Research issues of reliability of information are significant, and because messages can be posted anonymously (or with a deceptive "return address") to newsgroups, they are an unreliable tool for serious research, unless the goal of the research is to gain a sense of public opinion on a given topic. Having said that, newsgroups are a way of tapping into one of the largest resources for information on the Internet.

In order to read newsgroups, you need two things: the Internet address of a news server and newsreader client software for your computer. You will need to ask your ISP for the Internet address of a news server that you can use. Your ISP may even provide you with newsreader client software or at least tell you where you can get it.

Access to a news server is also called a newsfeed. Although a news server is a central location for reading newsgroups, there are actually many news servers. Each ISP may provide a news server for customers, but each one is usually a mirror, or a duplicate, of any other news server.

Newsgroup Naming Conventions. Each newsgroup has a specific name that follows a particular standard. The more popular topics may have more than one newsgroup dedicated to them, following a semilogical breakdown of topics. It is very important to understand the names of the newsgroups in order to identify ones that may interest you, as well as to identify the correct group for posting messages.

Newsgroups start with an abbreviated name that indicates, in general, the type of group it is. New ones are created from time to time, but the following is a list of the kinds seen most often:

alt	Generally accepted as meaning "alternative," these groups do not fit easily into the other categories. These groups may also not be available to all news servers, as they are more readily limited to geographic location or system.
biz	business-related topics
comp	computer- or technology-related topics
misc	miscellaneous topics that do not fit into the other categories
news	general information and announcements
rec	recreational activities, hobbies, and the arts
sci	scientific discussions
soc	social issues
talk	discussion and debates (Although discussion certainly takes place in other groups, the "talk" groups are specifically devoted to it.)

In addition to the top-level description, the names continue to become more specific. The more popular topics have multiple discussion groups devoted to various aspects of the topic. This keeps the amount of postings in any one group down and allows for better selection of groups. For an example in social history, the following groups are available:

soc.history
soc.history.living

soc.history.medieval
soc.history.moderated
soc.history.science
soc.history.war.misc
soc.history.war.us-civil-war
soc.history.war.us-revolution
soc.history.war.vietnam
soc.history.war.world-war-ii
soc.history.what-if

Newsreader Applications. Newsgroups can be reached by a variety of different client applications called newsreaders. For UNIX users, *rn* and *tin* are two examples of newsreader client applications. Other examples include *NewsWatcher* for the Macintosh and *Agent* for Windows-based systems. Recent versions of Web browsers like Netscape's Navigator and Microsoft's Internet Explorer include newsreader software in their package.

Depending upon your software, you may be given a choice to select from the full list of newsgroups when you begin. This is a massive list, so be sure to look for a search function to help find a particular newsgroup. You would then be allowed to create some kind of a customized list of only the newsgroups you want to follow.

Once you have selected a newsgroup to view, you will be able to see all the messages, subjects, and threads. The application you use should have a menu of available choices, such as the menu at the bottom of the screen in *tin*.

Advantages and Disadvantages of Newsgroups. One of the main advantages to newsgroups is the vast array of topics that are covered. The old phrase "something for everyone" certainly applies to newsgroups.

Because newsgroups do not send mail to your incoming mailbox, the problem of storing and reading through your own mail is not an issue, as it is with mailing lists.

Newsgroups seem to be undergoing a kind of growing pain. With more and more new users accessing the Internet everyday, the netiquette rules are constantly being repeated so that everyone is reminded. It is sometimes alarming to find a newsgroup that either has nothing at all to do with the stated topic or find annoying, junk-mail advertising or spam (i.e., "MAKE A HUNDRED DOLLARS A DAY!!") cross-posted to multiple groups. Depending upon your topic and your perspective, the fact that newsgroups invite and welcome a less formal tone of discussion could be both a good and bad aspect. However, this less formal tone also invites more flaming and uncivil behavior.

Still, newsgroups are an old tradition for the relatively young Internet. Nowhere else will you find such a gathering of minds representing the entire spectrum of human experience and interest. Using newsgroups as an information tool requires some patience and backbone, the ability to weed out all the "noise" and find the information if necessary. Often, it is information that you could not find as easily, given that finding as large a forum for discussing it is difficult.

Telnet and Remote Access

The ability to use a local computer (the one in front of you) to operate a computer or computer system at a remote location is one of the main functions of Internet life. Remote access gives an enormous range to research and allows use of computer resources from a considerable distance.

Telnet and remote access are technically slightly different, but they use similar protocols to accomplish the same thing. Remote access is also sometimes used to mean a dial-up connection, using a modem and telecommunications software from your local (client) workstation to reach a larger (server) computer that handles Internet protocols. Here we are concerned with a connection already made to the Internet and the subsequent use of remote resources by means of the Telnet protocol.

A Telnet connection can be used to search a library's catalog, examine databases, or look through archives. Using Telnet, you can connect to another computer where you already have an account and use that account as if you were sitting in front of that machine itself.

The use of Telnet and remote access will doubtless decrease as the Web and GUI browsers take on an ever greater share of network resources, but even these browsers often must incorporate Telnet capability to reach some resources. Luckily, Telnet is one of the easier Internet protocols to master, and some understanding of its operation may improve your own results, especially when problems arise.

How to Use Telnet

The Telnet protocol is relatively simple and employs a short list of commands. In contacting a Telnet host (server), one initiates the Telnet function, usually in one of two ways. If you are logged in to your ISP shell account, by typing "telnet" at your network prompt, followed by the address of the remote machine you wish to contact, you can reach the remote destination. In other environments you must launch whatever Telnet application you have (Trumptel is common for Windows, NCSA for Macintosh) from your local computer and designate the Internet address of the remote host. For example if I am at my account at San Francisco State University, my Telnet command to connect with the library catalog Melvyl of the University of California would look like this:

apollo% telnet melvyl.ucop.edu

where "apollo" is the name of the machine I am using, and the command "telnet" invokes the Telnet protocol software and the address of my destination, which has the familiar Internet convention of machine name, domain, and type. The Telnet software contacts the address, indicating that a user wants to make a Telnet connection, and if all goes well the remote (host) system will reply by requesting a name to log in with and perhaps request other information, such as what kind of terminal you are using (almost always a VT100). Long before Gopher and way before the Web, this was often the only way to use remote resources.

Publicly available resources often require that you log in as "guest" or "visitor," although sometimes other simple login names are chosen. For example, the history archives at the University of Kansas require that guests log in with the name "history":

apollo% telnet raven.cc.ukans.edu
login: history

A major characteristic of Telnet to remember is that when you log in to a remote computer, in effect you then must use that computer's operating system. This can be considerably disconcerting when it is an entirely unfamiliar system and none of your old standby commands have the slightest effect on the remote machine. Once connected, you are bound to the commands and conventions of the system to which you have connected. If it is a system that uses UNIX as an operating system, then only UNIX commands will work from your end. This sometimes calls for considerable flexibility and adaptability on the part of the researcher, but in practice often only a handful of Telnet resources are utilized for a given project, and the time taken to learn their peculiarities and command structure is not excessive. Often the initial login screen at the remote host will have a list of important commands or conventions, the most important being logoff instructions. A good habit is to make note of these instructions or perhaps use your "print screen" command locally to save the information in hard copy in your notebook for use after your short-term memory has lapsed.

Most machines that make themselves available to the public will not be impossible to use, but the responsibility is still yours to play by the rules of the host machine. You knocked on the front door and gained access; now you must follow the house rules of the operating system.

To cancel a Telnet session, the "Cont-]" sequence (hold control key down while pressing the right bracket symbol "]") will break the connection with the host and put you back at your Telnet prompt. This is often handy if you are unable to navigate a strange operating system or your screen "freezes" or some other network problem surfaces. On shell accounts, this will dump you back at the "telnet" prompt (telnet>), where the protocol is still active but the connection to the troublesome host has been terminated. You can then either close the Telnet session by typing "close" and then "quit" or by opening another connection by typing "open" and adding the Internet address of the desired remote site.

Research Applications

Telnet sites can include a range of material, although many of the tools previously only available through Telnet, such as library catalogs, have largely been replaced by Web based resources. Large catalogs, like the catalog of the University of California or the Library of Congress, are often useful to find rare or difficult-to-locate books and other resources. When conducting a research project of any depth, your local resources may not be equal to the task and some early reconnaissance on your part to determine what sorts of publication have been done in a particular area can be useful to help decide the next step of your research. Many times a book can be borrowed by Interlibrary Loan at your local library. University catalogs can also be useful for locating material like doctoral dissertations or other nonstandard items. Other useful sites can include databases of varied information and other kinds of archives.

FTP

FTP, which stands for File Transfer Protocol, allows the copying of one file or groups of files from one computer to another, regardless of type. There are two kinds of FTP we will be talking about: anonymous FTP and local FTP. Anonymous FTP allows a guest to log in to a remote host computer and copy files available to the public. These copied files are transferred to the guest's account, where they may be read or otherwise used. Local FTP allows the transfer of files from an Internet server to a floppy disk or home hard drive.

In practice, anonymous FTP was an enormous breakthrough because files could migrate across great distances and across platforms or operating systems. Researchers in Maine could share data or documents with their colleagues across the country in Oregon. A series of standardized commands were created, which allowed the host computer and the remote user to speak the same language. Although one of the drawbacks of FTP remains that it is not possible to "see" the files before transferring them, it remains a vital Internet function, and many documents and files found nowhere else can be accessed in FTP archives.

The commands to launch FTP are not impossible in and of themselves, but it is easy for new users to become intimidated or lost during the process of a transfer. As with the other Internet protocols we have used, only about a half-dozen commands are essential enough to memorize. The rest can exist in a cheat sheet or reference work for easy referral. To start a session, in your ISP shell account, type: FTP [host address] at the system prompt.

To use the fine FTP archive at Dartmouth, the process would look like this:

```
apollo% ftp ftp.dartmouth.edu
   Connected to ftp.dartmouth.edu.
   220-
   220- Welcome to the Dartmouth College FTP Server.
   220-
   220- Unauthorized or illegal use of this archive is prohibited.
   220- Send comments or complaints to ftp-admin@ftp.Dartmouth.EDU.
   220-
   220- Your hostname and userid are logged for all transfers.
   220- If you object to that, please disconnect now.
   220-
   220-
   220- webster.dartmouth.edu FTP server (Version wu-2.4.2-academ
       [BETA-13](1) Fri May 30 16:01:56 EDT 1997) ready.
Name (ftp.dartmouth.edu:fielden): anonymous
   331 Guest login ok, send your complete email address as password.
Password: fielden@sfsu.edu
```

The directory structure will be similar to the file structures you are familiar with at your own system. A root directory divides into smaller subdirectories, and usually each publicly accessible FTP site has a directory called "pub," which is the directory housing files made available to all visitors. Not all directories and files are public, however, and it is quite possible to navigate through an FTP archive and be prohibited from retrieving an appealing-looking file. The message received when trying to get a non-public file is usually "permission denied" and could be the result of a number of causes, including the use of that file by members at that site, sensitive nature of the material, lack of copyright clearance, etc.

Once connected, to view the contents of the root directory:

```
ftp> ls
    200 PORT command successful.
    150 Opening ASCII mode data connection for file list.
    Bin
    etc
    pub
    .afs
    people
    incoming
    outgoing
    Students
    ls-lR
    INDEX.gz
    dartmouth
    INDEX
    README

    226 Transfer complete.
    102 bytes received in 4.2 seconds (0.024 Kbytes/s)
```

Change to directory "pub":

```
ftp>cd pub
```

List contents of directory (-CF command compresses the listing).

```
ftp> ls -CF
    200 PORT command successful.
    150 Opening ASCII mode data connection for /bin/ls.
    Dante/          Renal-Function/    csmp-digest/    majordomo-docs/
    Exceptions/     SOP/               fedjobs@        prologue-users/
    Hyperbooks/     ScoutTracker/      floods/         protein/
    LLTI-IALL/      Students@          friends/        ptsd@
    PTSD/           VWPROJ/            gnuplot/        security/
    README          balaton@          mac@            software/
    226 Transfer complete.
```

Transfer the file "README" (case is important) to my account.

ftp>get README

Close and quit.

ftp>quit

File Types

There are two types of files when it comes to the Internet: text, or "ASCII" (American Standard Code for Information Interchange), and binary, everything else. A text file is any document created using only the 256 ASCII characters developed as an international standard. Most email is ASCII, and any document created using a simple text editor (Notepad in Windows, Simpletext in Macintosh, *pico* or *vi* in UNIX) is plaintext. These documents do not include graphics or anything that cannot be represented by characters not found on a standard computer keyboard. All other files, be they picture or sound files, movies, software or other executable files, even documents created in a word processor like Word, are binary. These include data that cannot be represented entirely by ASCII characters, and in the case of word-processed documents, include formatting commands that make them binary.

The default setting for anonymous FTP is ASCII, so one must specify binary before transferring a nontext file. One of the problems that sometimes arises when visiting an FTP site is determining the file type. Generally conventions exist to identify file types by the use of extensions appended to the end of a filename. Thus a file with the name of thesis.txt would be a text file, and cathedral.jpg can be identified as a "JPEG" (for Joint Photographic Experts Group) file, an image file in the JPEG format. Frequently FTP sites include compressed or archived files. Because disk space is at a premium, these files are collapsed to take up less room and must be transferred as binary files then "unpacked" at your end to be usable. Thus it is quite possible to find a file compressed by some utility that does not exist on your own machine, basically making that file worthless to you. Standardization is improving however, and more often files are compressed in a way that is most likely to be usable to visitors.

Transfer of these two file types requires different protocols, and it is necessary for you to specify file type when performing a transfer.

Other FTP Applications

Besides anonymous FTP on the Internet, other systems exist to copy files from one location to another. Although the dominance of the World

Wide Web and the growth in power and flexibility of Web browsers like Netscape has vastly simplified downloading documents of all types, there are a variety of FTP applications that permit easy transfer of files. Macintosh machines often make use of a freeware program called Fetch; Windows machines frequently use a program called WSFTP. Each of these graphics-based programs uses two sets of visual windows to identify the location and structures of host directory and local directory. Files to be transferred are highlighted with the cursor, choice made for means of transfer (ASCII or binary), and direction of transfer indicated with a button. With a network connection the download or upload can occur quite rapidly.

Increasingly, these applications have a central role in creating Web pages. After an initial document has been created in HTML format, it must be uploaded to a place on the Web server's hard disk, where it is then available for viewing by the Internet public.

World Wide Web

Origins

The World Wide Web is not very old, dating back to only 1989. Its growth has been phenomenal, outstripping all other Internet arenas in the last few years. This growth is what has caused the general public to become aware of the Internet as an entity and as a current phenomenon to be reckoned with. Many people mistakenly think that the World Wide Web itself is the Internet, but it is merely a subset, however large and pervasive, of the international network.

The initial proposal for the Web was written by Tim Berners Lee and represented a response to one of the problems that existed for the researchers at CERN, the European center for high energy physics study. For many subject areas, notably scientific disciplines, currency of information is of paramount importance. Advances in research are often made so quickly that by the time a research paper is published in an academic journal, the information is likely to be outdated or superseded by new discoveries. Thus other researchers, who depend on the journals for their information, are not kept as well informed as they might prefer. The original plan was to come up with a method to make documents and research results more quickly available to other researchers without the time delay of normal publication.

The plan was built on work done much earlier dealing with hypertext, which allowed one document to be linked by means of a "pointer" to another document. Several documents could be connected by links at appropriate context-suitable points. One usage of hypertext involved the reading of a typical high-level research paper, which in standard academic form made numerous footnote references to earlier research documents. If links were provided at the footnotes, the reader could jump from the original document to the footnoted document, saving the step of having to look up the footnoted work and retrieve it. With hypertext, a "web" of documents could be created, with the first document making branching connections to related documents.

NeXT did the development work, and by late 1990 network access to hypertext files was possible. CERN debuted the World Wide Web (often abbreviated as WWW or W3) in 1991, and the stage was set for the next major development. Although the original intent was to link mostly text documents, there was no reason pointers could not be set to nontext files as well and links established to a wide range of different file types.

The NCSA (National Center for Super-Computing Applications) in Urbana-Champaign, Illinois, developed, with the work of student Marc Andreessen, an application that took advantage of many of the features of the Web and added its own benefits. The new application was called Mosaic, and it was a front-end interface that combined a "browser" that could deal with the Web and its documents written in the markup language HTML (an outgrowth of another markup language, SGML) along with a handful of other tools to handle a variety of file formats. This first attempt at a grand unified interface incorporated various other applications to view image files (which cannot be interpreted by plaintext editors), as well as sound and other kinds of files. Mosaic was a Graphic User Interface, or GUI, and very quickly turned the world on its head.

Mosaic exploited the Web's potentiality for multimedia and turned out to be a simple way for even inexperienced Internet users to navigate the Web without having to learn all the various Internet protocols discussed at length in this book. By 1993 the impact of Mosaic had established a critical mass as more and more people experimented with its novel approach to Internet usage.

For some time Mosaic was the province only of those with direct Internet connections because the speed of data transfer required by large nontext files demanded more than what a standard dial-up connection could easily deliver. Development work and availability of SLIP (Serial Line Internet Protocol) or PPP (Point-to-Point Protocol) connections that improve dial-up connection speed and flexibility has grown however, and all ISPs now make them available for subscribers.

Andreessen graduated and moved on to form Netscape, which at one point produced the dominant Web browser, Navigator, although furious work has been done by Microsoft, with its Internet Explorer, and various other companies to make the "killer" browser for the Web. The current version of Netscape is fast and powerful and has many features not present in the early incarnations of Mosaic.

Browsers

Web browsers are applications that allow maximized use of the files found on the World Wide Web's network of servers. There are text-only browsers, like the application "Lynx" found on many UNIX machines. These permit navigation throughout the Web but lack the ability to view pictures or use other nontext files. Many times, however, when speed is paramount or when transfer capabilities are limited (as when using a slow modem or otherwise limited dial-up connection to an Internet provider), these are fine. But the browser Mosaic, with its ability to decipher a multitude of files, has spawned further refinements in the browser wars, and now Netscape's latest version (currently 6.0) competes with the research and development engineers at Microsoft as they employ the latest version of their browser, Internet Explorer. While the notion of an absolutely "seamless" interface, i.e., an application that moves effortlessly from location to location, file to file, is still a bit elusive, such enormous progress has been made that the earlier whiz-kid application of Internet life, the Gopher, has nearly disappeared.

GUI browsers such as Netscape permit easy, intuitive navigation. Large, easy-to-read buttons are activated by using a mouse to move a cursor arrow and "click" a button or by using the Enter key. Various toolbars indicate the Internet location of the file in question (the URL) and incorporate mechanisms to store frequently used URLs to revisit easily time and time again. Downloading (although not uploading) files is also simple, as is viewing the document source code in HTML. Printing is possible from the browser, and multiple configurations can be set up to employ other applications (plugins) to view movies, send mail, visit newsgroups, or utilize other files.

This attempt at an intuitive interface has made life simpler for many people who were unfamiliar with computer technology. With an easy navigation system, the memorization and utilization of cryptic UNIX commands is bypassed (or, more accurately, effectively translated). This simplification has also benefited those with mobility, sight, or other impairments. The democratic benefits to good browser design are impressive and welcome.

Research Aspects

The Web has intriguing elements for research. The ability to combine pictures and other formats with text, all delivered on a computer screen

San Francisco State University Library — Webpage for San Francisco State University Library with simple graphics and Hyperlinks (©1998 San Francisco State University).

with easy methods of downloading the data, is a wonderful boon to those seeking information. The ease with which documents may be made available (and people can create home pages in an extremely short amount of time) frees information dissemination from virtually all spatial and temporal limitations. The fertility of the human spirit is reflected in the astonishing output the Web makes possible, with a huge range of topic areas reflected, everything from contemporary culture to educational technology to literary criticism.

The blessing is not without its curse, however, and one of the great boons of the Web is also one of its liabilities— the sheer magnitude and range of material. Whereas libraries and other organizations whose mission is to preserve, organize, and present for use various information resources take seriously the need to arrange material carefully so that it may be found and used, this is not true for the Internet in general or for the Web in particular.

Finding what you want on the Web may take some doing. The lure may be irresistible, and the results either highly gratifying or teasing, but surfing for information is not the same as taking a systematic approach.

Certain kinds of information are well represented on the Web, some of which have been mentioned in the section "The Internet as a Research Tool" (see page 31). The commercial potential of the Web has served as an impetus for a great deal of marketing (if not downright advertising) information, and companies have climbed over one another attempting to disseminate information that suggests that their own company is superior, improved, a good investment opportunity, etc.

Information about companies, institutions, universities, and other entities is increasingly available on the Web. For this kind of information, the various search engines tend to work very well as locating aids. In particular, the URL of a given site frequently includes the company or institutional name or some abbreviation of it, as is the case with San Francisco State University's URL at http://www.sfsu.edu/ and with the Internal Revenue Service at http://www.ustreas.gov/.

The Web furnishes some advantages to research in a number of areas:

- *Ease of Navigation*: The ability to utilize one kind of searching mechanism (a Web browser) makes for a standardization of procedure. One set of search commands is easier to learn than dozens. Although this goal is not yet realized, enormous progress has taken place in the last few years.

- *Ease of Retrieval*: The Web browser's ability to download documents is extraordinarily easy to use, far surpassing the powerful but complicated FTP processes that existed as underlying structures in the Internet.

- *Contributions to Education through Self-Publication*: Teachers, instructors, faculty, and specialists are all able to publish their material on the Web easily. Course syllabi, notes, reading lists, photographs and charts, and sound and movie files— all can be set up on a Web page and made available to students or others who may benefit from the information. Additionally, publication of journal articles and other original works online can improve their dissemination to the scholarly community.

Web Finding Tools

Luckily, there is more than one attempt at work to make sense out of this chaos, with varying results. The index Yahoo!, which was developed by two Stanford graduate students and has since gone "public" with stock offerings, sets up a range of subject areas, with useful subcategories and lists of valuable resources. Various "search engines" that employ comput ers' remarkable abilities to match keyword queries with documents are also options for locating relevant material. These are maintained by a variety of organizations including major hardware manufacturers, software companies, and even experimental prototypes designed by students and other researchers.

For more information on the specifics of World Wide Web searching, look at the section on Internet Search Services in the Information Retrieval chapter on page 101. Comparing search engines is a fairly hot topic in the literature, and for competitive reviews see the bibliography.

It is important for the researcher to remember that unlike highly structured databases that follow traditional cataloging practices developed over many years by the library community, the searching indexes and search engines of the Internet are only beginning to evolve. Although there is some reason to expect foraging life to improve (improved standards for documents, enhanced search retrieval features), the economic advantages of such improvements are only just now being realized, and the Internet does not yet have a collection of information well ordered enough to be searched in an organized fashion. Combined with the impermanence of many resources and the lack of decent authority control, these factors can make Internet searching a highly frustrating and problematic endeavor.

Electronic Journals

An electronic journal is a journal, magazine, or newsletter published by electronic means. These can be available in several ways, notably by email, FTP or Web site. They possess most of the components we normally expect in conventional journals: editor, contributed articles, a distribution system, and, increasingly, advertising.

Some obvious advantages of electronic journals include currency of information, since the normal time lag from submission of article to publication can be minimized; ease of distribution, since with no physical attributes (bound volumes, stacks of paper, etc.) a complete middle step of publication is eliminated; and price (see previous example). Many journals are in fact free, although they can be difficult to find on the Internet.

One would think that electronic journals would benefit from many of the advances of Internet communication. Information could be disseminated quickly and directed at the people who might need it most essentially, keeping selected audiences informed and connected with their field. In practice, however, several things keep electronic journals from flourishing on the Internet, the most important of which is money.

Normal journals require a fair amount of capital to stay in business. Even scholarly academic journals, which tend to pay contributors only small sums of money, still must have a board of directors and reviewers, as well as editors and all the other trappings of publication. Unlike mainstream journals, which rely much more on advertising for working capital than subscription sales, they often must generate most of their revenue from donations and subscriptions. Although electronic publication may eliminate some of the costs of distribution, maintaining an adequate revenue remains a major issue. Whereas some journals, such as the *Chronicle of Higher Education*, make their online versions available free to regular subscribers, others require subscription payment before providing passwords to their online electronic versions. Many newspapers, such as the *San Francisco Chronicle*, have a noncomprehensive online presence, which may include main stories and selected columnists' work. They realize the importance of online accessibility yet do not want to make the entire contents of their paper available for free. Many other journals that might like to provide electronic access shy away from the second great dilemma of electronic journals: copyright issues.

Articles in journals, like material produced in books or anywhere else, are copyrighted and may not be duplicated except under the fairly strict provisions of fair use, as outlined in our section on legal issues. The extreme ease of electronic duplication has inhibited publishers from making their work available online because the chances of seeing their efforts get copied and distributed far and wide without receiving any compensation is considerably higher than in conventional situations. Until publishers can find a method for safe, secure payment for their work, electronic journals will not be as widespread as might be expected.

Despite these drawbacks, a number of electronic journals are available, and these should not be neglected by researchers.

Finding Electronic Journals

Finding electronic journals in your area of interest can be done in several ways. If you have a particular journal in mind, the easiest way is to use a Web search engine like AltaVista and enter the journal name as a search term. If the journal has an online presence, you should receive an address or a way to link to the journal. Many journals provide only a sample of their work online, but often that is enough to be useful. If they have a mechanism for subscribing to an online version, it will be outlined at the journal's home page.

Many journals are listed at Internet indexes like Yahoo!, and The World Wide Web Virtual Library site (http://www.e-journals.org/) has an extensive list of electronic journals.

Some subject disciplines are better represented than others. A special category of electronic journals called "zines" tends to be oriented toward current events and popular culture. Zines also tend to be irreverent, radical, highly idiosyncratic, and geared for amusement rather than research. However, they represent a window into Internet culture for the trendsetting online crowd and are a distinct phenomenon of the rapid growth of the Internet. An index of zines can be found at (http://www.zinebook.com/rec-ord.html).

The notion of self-publication has occurred earlier in our discussion of the World Wide Web, and it is worth noting here that despite the drawbacks of an online presence for traditional journals, the lure and ease of publication is irresistible to many who might not normally be part of publishing. Electronic journals can represent a mechanism for extensive dissemination of information of all varieties, and the initial investment in money may not be great, although the time commitment can easily be extensive.

The academic world depends on scholarly publishing to a great degree, for information dissemination and because most academic positions demand publication for tenure and retention for their faculty members, and will very likely find better ways to utilize electronic journals in the future. For scholarly research, publication normally requires that the submitted article be reviewed by a board of peers in the field before being accepted for publication, and there is no reason why this process would be any different for an electronic publication. Yet many faculty still remain attached to traditional methods of publication, not placing electronic publication in the same category. Until peer review becomes a more integral part of electronic journals, their use by academics will be limited.

Internet Culture

Internet Communication

One stage of research is information gathering. One of the easiest ways we gather information is simply to discuss and exchange ideas with other people: teachers, colleagues, friends, or even enemies. Human communi-

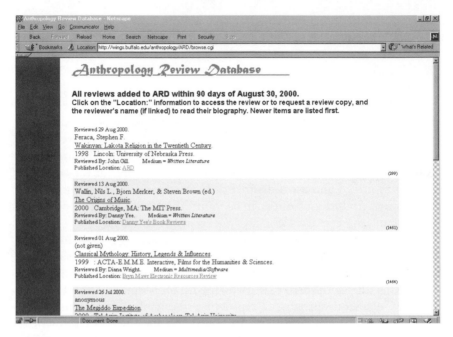

Anthropology Review — An online electronic journal at *http://wings.buffalo.edu/
anthropology/ARD/*.

cation is a fascinating and complex process. We communicate with each
other by a variety of methods, processing auditory, textual, and visual clues
to understand one another. Probably the richest form of communication
is a face-to-face conversation. During conversation, we consider the content, the emotional tone of the delivery, physical clues from facial expressions and hand gestures, perhaps even olfactory or tactile aspects, if, for
example, your fellow human puts a hand on your shoulder while speaking
to you.

Other forms of communication possess only a portion of the whole
spectrum of communication methods. The phone is purely auditory (unless
supplied with a teletypewriter, or TTY, connection for the hearing-impaired).
Handwritten letters are textual and visual but still capture some idosyn-
cratic elements of the person who wrote the letter. The size and expression
of the letters and the visual layout of the letter all contribute to a sense of
the person who created the communication. In addition, the level of interactivity varies with different forms of communication. A telephone
conversation allows instant interactivity, whereas a letter exchange involves
a time lag.

Some people are more comfortable with telephone calls than with letter writing. Of those people who prefer letter writing, some may write longhand with pencil and paper, whereas others may use computers. Communication over the Internet can present unique challenges. Understanding the differences and appreciating the limitations of various forms of communication on the Internet are important components to using it effectively.

Text-based "Conversation"

Visual, auditory, and tactile communication clues are, for the most part, missing in Internet communication. Recent advances in the technology provide us with a means to transmit graphical images, video, and even sound clips. However, the primary means of communication on the Internet between individuals and groups is textual. Email, for example, is usually purely "text-based." There is nothing except the typed words that appear on the screen for both sender and recipient. Even the typeface, or font, is dictated by the equipment you are using. An email message from one person will look about the same as an email message from anyone else, whether it is a personal letter or an assignment from a supervisor or an instructor. For most Internet communication content is everything.

In the world of corporate communication, for example, memoranda are sent back and forth. Tone and content of a memo from a supervisor or colleague is usually straightforward and nonambiguous. However, on the Internet, this form of communication can sometimes present difficulties. The Internet grew out of a research environment, with an attitude of acceptance towards the free flow and informal sharing of information and ideas. The absence of visual or other clues and the typical delay for messages to be sent and received (and read) can easily inhibit understanding. In particular, emotional tone and relatively subtle aspects of communication such as sarcasm or parody may escape the reader, especially if the message is read quickly or carelessly.

This situation has led to some interesting conventions among those who frequently use the Internet for communication. A whole arsenal of "clues" indicating emotional tone or other qualities has been invented. Mostly used in the informal communications that are the basis for much of the information sharing on the Internet, these clues flesh out the communication. Among them is the infamous profusion of smileys or emoticons (**emotional icons**) that many insert into text-based messages. The most common example of one of these nontext clues is often used to indicate amusement and can be inserted into a message, like so: :-). When one rotates the page (or your head, if you are looking at a computer screen) 90 degrees to the right, the punctuation marks appear as a human face smiling and suggest that the writer was amused while composing the message. Other sample emoticons include the following:

    :-)   smiling
    ;-)   winking
    :-(frowning
    =:-0   surprised

Another peculiarity of Internet users is the widespread use of abbreviations and acronyms to represent common phrases or concepts. For example, "BTW" means "by the way," and "FAQ" stands for "Frequently Asked Questions." One could argue that this practice arose out of either laziness or bad typing skills: nevertheless, it is common enough in discussion groups and mailing lists that it should at least be recognized. Some other common examples:

    AFK   Away from keyboard
    B4   Before
    FYI   For your information
    IMHO   In my humble opinion
    RTFM   Read the fine manual

If you spend any time at all on the Internet, you will see these peculiar characters that, at first, look like typographical errors. Although they are most often represented in whimsical and informal arenas, and some of them are quite funny, it is important that you understand their purpose. With communication being limited to the 101 or so keys on a keyboard, Internet users have developed emoticons to convey emotional tone of a message and acronyms to get their message across quickly. However cumbersome or grammatically incorrect these clues are, their existence suggests at least the occasional need among many Internet users to amplify their message by nonconventional textual means.

In addition, a sizable vocabulary of words and usages unique to Internet culture has been coined. Internet users have invented phrases such as "smileys" and "netiquette" and adopted terms like "flame" and "spam" to represent ideas or actions. Although at times these terms and their use may seem silly, they are accepted terms for discussion throughout the Internet.

Text-based communication calls for the highest possible degree of precision in the use of language. When a message is likely to be seen by dozens, if not hundreds or thousands of others, the need for clear, nonambiguous language is paramount. The words you type are the only evidence that the Internet world has for understanding your message. Clear language has the dual advantage of increasing the probability of achieving one's own communication needs by clearly stating the issue, as well as minimizing the potential for follow-up clarifications, retractions of inferred slights or insults, and general misunderstandings.

"Netiquette"

The term "netiquette" was derived by a combination of the words "network" and "etiquette" to suggest the conventions of the interactions of humans on the network. In general, the conventions parallel those of any other social world but possess a few idiosyncrasies and unusual terms. Like all other social conventions, netiquette does not eliminate social friction, but it does provide a framework of acceptable behavior. Often those who disregard netiquette out of sheer orneriness are ostracized by the community, which is one way that Internet communities police themselves.

Many of those who participate in Internet life have noted the similarity of the Internet to other kinds of frontier communities. After all, the Internet is a relatively new world for large numbers of people and remains somewhat exotic. Its sheer size and growth precludes comprehensive exploration. Many of its early users were pioneers in the sense that their energy, problem-solving abilities, and intelligence, as well as their relatively small numbers and close-knit communities, all contributed to the development of greater access for others. Rules were made up as these pioneers went along. Even now people "discover" the Internet and return to fellow students, office mates, or spouses with stories of various information treasures found. As early as 1992, Clifford Lynch, then Director of Library Automation for the University of California, declared in a lecture that there probably was not a single office place in the country that had not "lost" someone to the Internet. Ed Krol, in his seminal book on the Internet *Whole Internet User's Guide and Catalog*, describes two essential characteristics of Internet life that parallel frontier values—individualism and preservation of the community.

These two apparently mutually exclusive tenets, and the tension they provide between individual freedom and survival of the Internet environment, help explain much of Internet culture. As explorers in this new world, individuals prize their freedom. Their ability to say anything, go anywhere, do anything, and even exploit everything in sight is often seen as a basic Internet right. Great debates have arisen over issues like censorship and whether there should be any restrictions at all on files and documents found at Internet sites. This sort of controversy has resulted in U.S. federal legislation designed to regulate the content of information on the Internet, but the debate is far from settled. At the same time that Internet citizens prize their individuality, however, they also realize the danger of catastrophe to their environment if certain safeguards are not adopted.

Like other frontier resources, early Internet sites could be fragile. Computers designed to handle a certain amount of network traffic could be overwhelmed by unexpectedly high use. Network communication, although built to be robust, cannot always tolerate the exponential growth that it now experiences. Hardware, software, cables, and gateways all have limitations. Internet citizens learned early on that it was important to protect their resources. Usage could not be greedy or unlimited, or there was a danger of the resources being dissolved, or, for some, the worse fear was that they would indeed become regulated to death. Individuals on the Internet needed a code of conduct that acknowledged their fierce individual freedoms but also ensured lasting availability and distribution of information resources.

Obviously, these principles of individualism and putting the network first will collide more than occasionally. Individualism is a much-valued human characteristic, and people often feel instinctively that their own desires have greater validity or importance than those of others. Friction can arise at several points when a new Internet user (or "newbie") arrives and, from ignorance, violates an Internet social convention. Like frontier saloons, disputes can escalate quickly, especially given the lack of more established "civilized" codes of conduct or formal governance.

The best-known example of a breach of netiquette is "flaming." A "flame" is an insulting or uncommonly aggressive email message directed at an individual or individuals. In general, a flame is characterized by a highly emotional tone and a tendency toward personal attack, ridicule, or derision. Its unfortunate frequency is perhaps due to the nature of electronic communication. People often feel free to say whatever comes into their heads, and the speed and ease with which a reply may be made to an email message makes it very easy for messages to be sent off thoughtlessly. There appears to be less restraint in sending aggressive messages over the Internet, probably due to a sense of anonymity and no immediate physical or confrontational threat. Unfortunately, coping with flaming behavior is only part of the problem. It is sometimes difficult to resist the temptation to flame back, which only continues the cycle of antagonism. The general commonsense rule is, when prompted by strong feelings to send a message of rebuttal to a provocative post, wait overnight. This is the online version of "thinking before speaking," and it is certainly never a bad idea in any situation. Keep in mind that once you send an email message, much like leaving a message on an answering machine, you cannot take it back.

Another email abuse is the practice known as "spamming." A "spam" is an overtly commercial message, usually advertising goods or services, that is sent to hundreds or thousands of people at a time. It is the Internet equivalent of junk mail, and many ISPs have specific rules against mass mailings. Spamming is viewed as worse than an annoyance and can result in the loss of your ISP services.

Copyright law makes the use of others' words or messages a serious offense. Before forwarding an email message to someone else, it is common courtesy to request permission from the author of the piece. This minimizes the danger of passing around information that might be regarded as personal or sensitive by the author and gives him or her the opportunity to control the destiny of the message. As the author of the message, you should remember how easily your email can be distributed. It is perhaps also helpful to realize that whatever you send as email can be, and probably is, archived and saved somewhere. It is best not to dispatch a message that you would not want to own up to at some later moment.

The Computer Ethics Institute, a think tank in Washington, D.C., developed the Ten Commandments of Computer Ethics in 1992. Although it is targeted for general computer usage, it can be applied quite readily to use of the Internet. Combined with existing laws governing intellectual property, privacy, and criminal activity, these commandments are a straightforward guide to Internet usage.

1. Thou shalt not use a computer to harm other people.
2. Thou shalt not interfere with other people's computer work.
3. Thou shalt not snoop around in other people's computer files.
4. Thou shalt not use a computer to steal.
5. Thou shalt not use a computer to bear false witness.
6. Thou shalt not copy or use proprietary software for which you have not paid (or been given authority to do so).
7. Thou shalt not use other people's computer resources without authorization or proper compensation.
8. Thou shalt not appropriate other people's intellectual output.
9. Thou shalt think about the social consequences of the program you are writing or the system you are designing.
10. Thou shalt always use a computer in ways that insure consideration and respect for your fellow humans.

The size and growth of the Internet demands some standards of conduct. In general, despite the proclivity toward individualism, most Internet users prefer it to continue to develop. This demands cooperation between users and a degree of civility in communication. Many communities realize that if they do not police themselves, it may not be long before someone will be doing it for them. Few communities can tolerate true chaos, and the Internet is no exception.

Participation on the Internet

Although reliable statistics on the number of Internet users are hard to find, it is safe to say that millions of people currently have access to it and that the number is rapidly growing. When you first start using the Internet, you will probably spend most of your time exploring and getting a feel for the new environment, its applications, and your own skills. You may spend time reading a newsgroup or subscribe to a mailing list (see Discussion Groups on page 72). Your individual presence may go unnoticed for the most part, and you would certainly not be alone. There is a silent majority of users on the Internet who use its resources for research, education, and recreation. The term used to describe these users who do not make much noise themselves is "lurkers," and it refers primarily to discussion group participants who do not contribute to a discussion. An example of this could be a mailing list with hundreds of subscribers, but you often see that the messages in the discussion come from a relatively small group of people. The silent ones are the lurkers, and they are doing the Internet equivalent of listening in on a conversation.

When you use the Internet to conduct research, you use the resources of the millions of individuals and organizations who distribute information and share ideas. Participating in a discussion or publishing your work on the Internet is not a requirement for use, but common sense, netiquette, and copyright law demand that you give credit and acknowledgment where they are due. If you use the Internet to find information, chances are very high that other people are interested in the same information (especially if you find results). If you post a message to a discussion group asking for information or requesting replies to a survey, you will often see replies to your message from other people interested in the same information you are gathering. If you get responses or results from your information request, you should make that information available to others who may be interested. There are many ways to do this: sending email to the group, creating a Web page, or writing a paper or a book. You must always keep in mind the rules and regulations regarding copyright and get permission or give credit where necessary.

4
Information Retrieval

Fundamentals of Electronic Searching

Introduction to Electronic Searching

Electronic searching means using the computer as a tool to locate and identify relevant research materials. At its most basic level, electronic searching does not differ substantively from more traditional methods like using the card catalog or print indexes at the local public library. In each case the researcher must have some idea of what he or she is looking for and must use a tool, electronic or otherwise, to locate and/or use relevant resources. Electronic searching involves searching a database, a collection of records that have something in common. Databases can be local, where access is restricted to one computer, or online, accessible over a network. A local database might be a collection of names and addresses you maintain on your own computer with a database program (like FileMaker Pro or Microsoft Access). Online databases, such as the types found on the Internet, usually contain a very large number of records. Examples of online databases include library catalogs and phone directories.

Persistent myths surround the use of computers and the Internet to find information. One is that the Internet makes finding information easier. In fact "easy" is a relative term when it comes to computers. As with almost everything, using computers and the Internet requires skill and practice. The more you do something, the easier it becomes. In general, technology has made it easier to gather and store large amounts of information, but retrieving that information requires some knowledge of how it is selected, stored, and arranged.

Another myth is that "everything" can be found on the Internet. This is especially untrue for research purposes. The volume of creative work that has been done over the centuries is much too vast to be put on the Internet. The use of computers in research can often be a step in the process, but the vision of the "paperless office" or the "paperless library" is far from reality.

Vast stores of knowledge and information are on the Internet, but locating exactly what you want requires some forethought about how to search for it. The power of computers to manipulate information is unquestionable, but harnessing it takes a substantial investment in time.

The goal here is not to turn you into an expert database searcher but to provide enough of a framework for you to be able to appreciate and use some of the unique elements of searching strategy for your own benefit when employing Internet resources. Many times it helps to know what you are dealing with, whether it is a real database or a loosely collected pile of information. As with most computer applications, some understanding of underlying structure allows you to appreciate both the strengths and limitations of your intended arena.

Advantages & Disadvantages of Electronic Resources

There are some obvious advantages to using the Internet for finding research materials. Some of these include:

- *Remote Access and Shared Use.* Unlike your local library, the Internet is available 24 hours a day, 7 days a week, regardless of where you are physically located, as long as you have a computer and a telecommunications connection. In addition, more than one user at any given time can have access, thereby sharing the resource. If you are using a book in a library, no one else can have access to that book until you are finished with it.

- *Currency of Information.* Print-based resources need to go to a printer and then be shipped. Electronic resources can be updated and made available in less time and are therefore more current than print-based resources. Some resources on the Internet are updated hourly or even more frequently.

- *More Sophisticated Searching.* Electronic resources allow more flexibility in searching. When you look in the phone book for a person's phone number, you need to know what city the person is in, and you can only find the person if you know his or her last name. A phone book on the Internet can be searched by last name, phone number, city, state, zip code, or a combination of methods. Additionally, print indexes take up lots of physical space and are usually published in a series of annual volumes. To search five years' worth of information, you may need to look in five different books. An online resource can search multiple years' worth of data with a single search. A researcher can develop a search strategy that includes several components and quickly zero in on relevant material.

- *Ease in Archiving.* When you find information on the Internet, you can usually save it immediately (or print it if you have an attached printer). Print-based information needs to be copied by hand or by using a copying machine (since tearing pages out of books is not recommended).

However, using the Internet for research is not the universal remedy for all research problems. Some of the disadvantages can include:

- *Dependence on Technology,* If the power goes out, the batteries die, the computer breaks, the phone line is disconnected, you get a busy signal, your ISP has network problems, a backhoe cuts through a network line, or any one of a myriad of possible technological-disaster scenarios occurs, you no longer have access to the Internet. Granted, these may only be temporary setbacks, but setbacks usually happen when least wanted.

- *Cost.* Owning a computer costs more than owning a library card. There are additional costs such as a modem, printer, ISP charges, etc. Luckily, your school, workplace, or local library probably provides access to the Internet.

- *Searching Skills Required.* As stated earlier, searching electronic resources for information requires skill and practice. A typical search statement for a database may look like this:

(technolog? or computer?) with (librar? or school?) not elementary

or

technolog* or computer* w/10 librar* or school* and not elementary

or

(technolog! | computer!) near (library! | school*) x elementary

(You should begin to see a pattern in the above searches).

Sometimes the power of electronic searching is overcome by the complexity or user-unfriendliness of its search commands and structure. The fundamentals covered in this section will provide you with a framework for evaluating and effectively using all types of databases.

- *Limited Archival Material.* Many databases of the type used for research were not created in electronic form until the 1970s. With the exception of material in the public domain, older material is often harder to find on the Internet.

Understanding the peculiarities of electronic searching is made easier if you compare it to searching print-based resources. You use print resources to find information all the time. Sometimes, you may do it for a specific assignment like a term paper or a proposal. Other times, you may consult print-based resources almost "unconsciously," as when you use a telephone directory or the index at the back of this book.

Traditional Print-based Searching

Traditionally, the search for research materials usually led one to the library. The library card catalog, long a feature of virtually all kinds of libraries, is probably the most familiar print-based index for most people. An index is a type of guide. At the back of this book is an index that tells you the topics covered herein and refers to them by page number. A card catalog is an index for an entire library. It tells you if a certain resource is part of that library's collection and refers to it (usually) by a call number. The organizational scheme is simple in concept though not always in execution. Material is organized by author, title, and subject. To find an item from a known author or a given title, one would consult the catalog under the appropriate category, note the call number, which is a location code, and using that code, go to the section of the library where the material is shelved.

Besides library card catalogs, a multitude of other printed indexes and other resources exist to deal with a wide variety of subjects and materials. Some are extremely specialized, concerning themselves with a narrowly defined subject discipline; others are wide-ranging and cover all types of information. Although sometimes cryptic in their use of abbreviations and codes (usually to save space and printing costs), they parallel the structure of library card catalogs in that the searchable categories are limited.

To use a print resource, the researcher consults the index or table of contents, which may be divided into separate categories. In the case of a journal or magazine index, once a topic is located, there will be a list of items, usually with a short description called a bibliographic record, which is similar to a card-catalog record. For journal indexes the record usually includes the standard author and title information and, more important, information on where the article was published, which includes the name of the journal, volume and number, date and page numbers of the article, all necessary to find the work. Some indexes go one step further and include an abstract, which is a short summary of the article's contents. This abstract is often valuable because it allows the researcher to better evaluate the work to determine whether it fits the needs of the research.

Readers' Guide to Periodical Literature is an index used for finding articles in general interest magazines and journals. It is issued approximately every two weeks and then a year's worth is issued as a cumulative index for the entire year. It has been in print since 1901, so there are nearly a hundred individual annual volumes.

ERIC (Educational Resources Information Center) is an index used for finding articles and reports found in magazines, journals, and other materials related to education. It is published monthly, with annual cumulations. It has been in print since 1966 and has over thirty individual annual volumes.

Hoover's Handbook of American Business is an annual directory listing large U.S. public companies, with brief descriptions of each company.

Familiar Quotations, often referred to as "Bartlett's Familiar Quotations," is a collection of famous (and not-so-famous) quotations from ancient and modern literature.

Figure 4.1: Examples of print-based resources

Once a sufficient list of resources is compiled, the researcher must then perform the second step of locating the material. Sometimes the library subscribes to the journal, in which case the researcher must locate the journal in the library, often in a separate area of the library reserved for journals, or periodicals as they are often known. If the journal is not available, three choices remain: purchase a copy of the issue for yourself (which can be expensive if the item is no longer in print), locate the journal in another nearby library, or request the item through the library's Interlibrary Loan service. Often this service is free or of minimal cost, and the main drawback is the wait for the article to be photocopied and sent to your local library.

Although printed indexes vary considerably in form, the concept remains universal: trying to put lists of similar items together to assist in their retrieval. Electronic indexes follow this principle as well.

Electronic Searching Basics

Using electronic resources to find research material is not much different from using print resources. In fact, many databases evolved out of long-standing print resources.

Readers' Guide to Periodical Literature is an index used for finding articles in general interest magazines and journals. It is available in electronic form from many commercial database providers.

ERIC (Educational Resources Information Center) is an index used for finding articles and reports found in magazines, journals, and other materials related to education. It is available on the Internet from *AskERIC* (http://ericir.syr.edu/), a database compiled and maintained by the U.S. Department of Education.

Hoover's Handbook of American Business is an annual directory listing large U.S. public companies, with brief descriptions of each company. It is available on the Internet (http://www.hoovers.com/) in both a free and enhanced, fee-based version.

Familiar Quotations, often referred to as "Bartlett's Familiar Quotations," is a collection of famous (and not-so-famous) quotations from ancient and modern literature. It is freely available on the Internet (http://www.columbia.edu/acis/bartleby/bartlett/).

Figure 4.2: Examples of electronic resources

Of course, there is the obvious difference of print vs. computer, but the process is essentially the same: once you identify a useful resource, you need to learn how to use it to find the information. It sounds simple, but the reality can get quite complicated.

The process of electronic searching requires a combination of two skills: understanding the research process and successfully utilizing an electronic database, which in itself is a form of computer literacy. A researcher needs to know what he or she is looking for and then must sift through the information available with an eye to its potential utility. The second component is a much more recent development in research skills and involves the successful query of a database. Neither component by itself will be sufficient — many traditionalists have great difficulty as online searchers due to their inability to learn the database command language and structure. On the other hand, people who are intimately familiar with database management and structure can get lost without some understanding of content and a means to evaluate data for reliability and utility.

The evaluative function is vital in these efforts. Many excellent online researchers regard the Internet with considerable horror. Databases are usually designed with a high degree of order, with a variety of fields that allow similar things to be grouped together. Searching can be done in an extremely precise manner that maximizes good results. The Internet is about as far from organized as is possible to get, and many of the good online searcher's tricks are challenged in such an amorphous environment.

Before tackling the peculiar problems of dealing with an unorganized but treasure-laden morass like the Internet, let us examine online searching in more detail.

Database Arrangement

The concept of electronic searching centers around the database. A database is a collection of records that are similar in some respect. Records are discrete units in a database; a database can have as many records in it as storage space will allow. Each record is complete in the information it contains with respect to the type of database you are searching. What is contained in these records depends on the type of database they are in. Records could be directory listings, bibliographic citations to articles or books, statistical data, or even the full text of a paper or book. In other words, if you are searching a database that is an index to journal articles, one article citation is a complete record. Generally speaking, each record is made up of fields, and each record in a single database has the same fields.

Although this may seem very basic, understanding how a database is arranged can help you to search that database effectively.

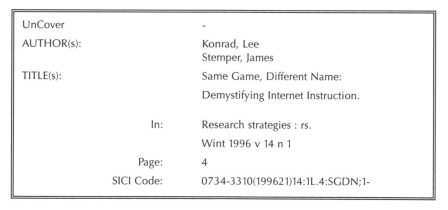

Figure 4.3: Sample database record from the *CARL Uncover* database.

Submitting Queries

In order to search an electronic resource, you must give the computer a set of instructions that will tell the database what you are looking for. This set of instructions is called a query. With a few notable exceptions, queries are not like the questions you would pose to a reference librarian. For example, you cannot type "Find me all the information on U.S. trading policies and practices with Japan."

The database software that allows you to give instructions to the computer and makes the computer understand the instructions is sometimes referred to as a search engine. Many advances have been made in the development of search engines, and every year producers claim to have made the software "easier" to use. As noted earlier, however, "easy" is a highly subjective term when it comes to computers and technology. Submitting queries, which is the topic of discussion in this section, is not always an intuitive process, and careful selection of search terms is necessary for good results. Besides the difficulty of queries, the databases can be extremely complicated, with various (nonstandardized) means of sorting, merging, and arranging information.

Most databases support some form of the following concepts for searching: keyword searching, Boolean search logic, truncation, or limiting.

The differences between one database and another usually have to do with the way they handle these concepts within the confines of a particular search engine. The differences usually boil down to differences in the interface, as in the case in all other kinds of software. Word processing software, regardless of manufacturer, allows you to create, edit, format, and print documents. Each version allows you to do that one procedure, but exactly how they do it is covered in a multitude of manuals and third-party books such as *The WordPerfect Handbook*. In other words, as long as you know what things are possible in database searching, then you only need to find out exactly how to do it in a particular database.

Keyword Searching

The first and most important step in electronic research is the careful selection of keywords. Keywords are the terms that uniquely define the subject matter you are researching. In the simplest possible terms, you provide a word or set of words, and the search engine tries to find matches, or "hits," documents or records that meet the requirements of your search query. In practice, things get considerably more complicated than this, but the most important concept to grasp is that the searching procedure is simply looking for words that match each other. The success of the operation will depend mightily on the choice of words submitted, and there is no magic search engine yet that can compensate for a poor choice of keywords.

A good way to start when deciding on keywords is to try to formulate your research project as a question or a simple statement:

What are the effects, if any, of television violence on children?

The next step is to identify all the words that define your subject:

What are the *effects*, if any, of *television violence* on *children*?

Then isolate those words:

effects
television
violence
children

These words form the basis of your search. You may, and probably will, modify them as you go along, but they are your starting point.

It is important to remember one very fundamental point about using computers for searching databases: computers can seem incredibly dumb. Although advances in artificial intelligence may claim otherwise, within the context of this book it is essential to understand the limits of technology when it comes to searching for research materials. Computers will only find what you tell them to find. What does this mean in searching?

If you search for:	The computer *will not* find:
effects	influence
television	tv
	t.v.
	cable
violence	aggression
children	kids
	child
	adolescents

For example, if the database you are searching is a full-text collection of newspaper articles, the statement "groups of *children* in the 14 and under age group were studied to evaluate the *effects* of *violence* portrayed on *television*" would match your search query and you could then view that record. However, the statement: "kids act as if they are under the influence of aggressive acts they have seen portrayed on T.V." would *not* match your search query, even though that record might be applicable to your research.

In other words, the computer will take your keywords quite literally. To a computer, "car" and "automobile" do not mean the same thing. Computers simply match strings of characters together and cannot make inferences based on uses of the language. The nuances of vocabulary — the fact that one word can mean several things in context, or many words can mean the same thing — are part of what makes a language rich. A computer, however, does not consider context when trying to match search queries. There are ways around this, but it is important to remember this facet of electronic searching.

An additional factor in the selection of keywords is the difference between words and phrases.

Keywords	*Phrase*
violence	television violence
television	

Depending on the database you are searching, a computer may or may not recognize two terms next to each other as a phrase and search them exactly as they appear. This varies among databases, but it is something to keep in mind when searching.

Although this searching method has some drawbacks, it harnesses one of the fabulous powers of computers, which are able to sift through enormous heaps of data quickly and accurately and retrieve records faster than any human could run through a library. In choosing keywords, be very specific in your selection, understand that a computer will not read any meaning into your search terms and that you may need to compensate for this.

Understanding Search Logic

Now that you have your keywords, can you type them in as a search query? No, not exactly. Identifying keywords is only the first step in searching an electronic resource. Instructing a computer by typing "effects television violence children" will not necessarily find relevant information. You need to tell the computer *how* you want those keywords to be found. This is normally done by combining the terms using search logic. Search logic is part of the instruction set you give to a computer; it allows you to specify exactly how you want keywords to be found and gives you a little control over the context in which they are found. This is where the computer's advantage of "more sophisticated searching" can really be found.

Having a functional knowledge of search logic takes practice and experience. Recognition of the manner in which computers are used for searching is a necessary precursor to the development of a query.

In particular, the ability to combine search terms together to form one query is lacking in printed indexes. If one wanted to examine the economic factors in the American Civil War for example, a hypothetical printed index would need to be consulted for two categories—American Civil War and some category of economic factors. The list provided by each might have records that fit into both categories, but very likely each list would contain a great many records that had to do with only one of these considerations. However, in an electronic environment, a search query can be formulated to include both concepts in one search, and the computer search engine will arrive at a simpler and more elegant result than most printed indexes can provide.

Combining Search Terms

Most search engines rely on "Boolean logic" to combine search elements. George Boole was a nineteenth-century American mathematician who worked with set theory and developed a symbolic notation for use in working with mathematical sets. His theories have survived into most modern search engines as the dominant method of combining search terms.

Development in "natural language processing" is progressing but not yet common. Natural language processing in databases allows you to enter a search query as a normal question:

Why does the moon look larger at the horizon?

These databases use complicated mathematical algorithms to analyze a sentence and assign "weights" to terms. Although the development is promising, the majority of databases available still use Boolean-based searching logic.

The Boolean operators, as they are often called, are connecting terms that are recognized by the computer doing the searching and that indicate how keywords should be combined. There are three major Boolean operators, usually represented by the three words: AND, OR, NOT.

These words should not be considered keywords. They are specific instructions to a search engine on how to combine keywords.

AND allows you to combine one search term with another, so that the search engine looks for matches that *include both terms*. For example, we could construct a search that looked like this:

violence and television

The search engine would find all records that contained the keyword "violence" as well as the keyword "television." Any records that did not possess both terms would not be selected.

OR is another way to combine search terms, but it is the opposite of AND. It is usually used to combine terms with similar meanings. It is used to find records that contain *either* of the keywords or *both* the keywords:

children or kids

The search engine would find all records that contain the keyword "children," as well as all records that contain the keyword "kids."

It should be obvious by now that the two operators mentioned so far have quite different results. AND is a term that creates a smaller, more narrowly defined set of records because both terms are required to be found within the records. OR is a term used to create larger more indiscriminate sets of records because only one of the terms must be present in a record. If we use the earlier example of "violence and television" and replace the AND with OR, we would get all records that contain the keyword "violence" or the keyword "television." This could be a huge set of records, depending upon the database.

The third Boolean operator is NOT, used to *exclude* certain search terms. This operator removes a keyword from consideration. If, for example, you were interested in television but not cable television, you could use the search statement:

television not cable

You would then retrieve records with the keyword "television," but records with the keyword "cable," even if they also include "television," would be excluded from your set of records.

The use of the NOT operator can be problematic. It is impossible to predict how a writer might choose to convey a particular message. For example, if you are looking for information on infections caused by a virus but not by bacteria, you may use the search statement:

virus not bacteria

However, if a record contains the sentences

> It was originally thought that this infection was caused by *bacteria*. However, further studies revealed the cause to be a *virus*.

your search would not retrieve it because you excluded records containing the keyword "bacteria."

Refining Search Terms

Many times in the course of research, one may pose a query and find that there appears to be nothing written on the topic. Although sometimes this is actually the case and one has stumbled upon an area completely devoid of study, very often the cause of this apparent result is a matter of terminology. Much of the terminology is dependent on the context of the information — what database one is looking in, what subject area is involved.

For example, "schizophrenia" is a highly technical term used and understood with a precise definition by psychologists. Other terms that one might be tempted to use, such as "split personality" or something equivalent, might not be used by the researchers producing the literature. This is a case where consulting with what is called "controlled vocabulary" would be extremely helpful.

Controlled vocabulary is defined as the terms *determined by the database producer* to be "official" terms for the representation of a particular subject. If the database uses the term "automobile" but you are typing in "car," then you may not find all the relevant articles in that database, even though the terms may mean essentially the same thing.

Those who study information retrieval have long known that locating documents blindly is a difficult process. If there is a document that is close to the kind of document desired, then an examination of its qualities often allows the researcher to construct a query that will result in retrieval of other similar documents, sometimes with good results. This sort of process works well in other arenas besides library catalogs as well. One difficulty is that often the controlled vocabulary is not available for consultation when one is creating a search, although many databases do possess an "online thesaurus" or index that allows one to examine synonyms. The Internet is nearly devoid of controlled vocabulary. Its sheer size alone limits any attempt to "catalog" its contents. Without such aid, the researcher must fall back on his or her skill in developing alternative search terms.

Alternative Terms

After you select your keywords, the second step is to develop alternative terms for each of your keywords. In this manner, if your first attempt to locate information fails, you will have alternative terms from which to construct a second search. One way to do this is simply to think of similar terms. These terms may not necessarily be synonyms. "Car" and "automobile" are two words that mean essentially the same thing. However, depending upon the context of your search, "computer" and "technology" may also mean the same thing, although they are not technically synonyms.

If you are looking for information on the use of computers in schools to enhance the education of children, you may select the following keywords:

computer
school
education
children

However, alternative search terms would include:

computer	school	education	children
technology	pre-school	learning	kids
internet	grade school	training	adolescents
	elementary school		students
	middle school		
	high school		
	college		
	university		

The search terms you select depend entirely on the context of your search. If you are, for example, only looking for applications of the Internet in elementary schools, you could rule out some terms. This is all part of refining the research process.

Another strategy is to consult a thesaurus or other listing of search terms. As mentioned, such aids are sometimes available online in the database itself, but often they cannot be viewed except at an appropriate library or archive. There are thesauri for many disciplines, but they vary considerably in precision. Overgeneralizing somewhat, the spectrum runs from very narrowly defined terms in the sciences to extremely broad and sometimes ambiguous terms in some of the humanities.

Truncation

Truncation is the process of using a symbol to allow the database to search for alternative spellings—a common phenomenon in language. You now understand that a computer cannot recognize that the keywords "automobile" and "car" are synonymous. However, in many cases a computer cannot recognize as similar keywords with variant spellings. Examples of this include:

color	colour (a British spelling)
library	libraries
farm	farmer
women	woman

The symbol used for truncation may vary from database to database, but the concept remains the same. If you type:

farm*

you will retrieve:

farm
farmer
farming
farms

This is an extremely valuable way to expand a search, sometimes taking you to areas you would not have thought about independently. This is essentially the same as typing in

farm or farmer or farming or farms

but it is a whole lot easier.

Occasionally there is a way to truncate a word internally, often called embedded truncation or wildcard searching. This is done by using a symbol within a word, such as

wom?n

This will retrieve:

women or woman

Again, you could just type in "woman or women," but truncation makes it much easier.

Possible symbols used in truncation include: !, #, $, *, and ?. Choosing which symbol to use depends on the database. When using one electronic resource extensively, it makes a lot of sense to locate and print out a listing of commands, such as truncation characters or other commonly used commands to keep by your workstation to consult while doing your research. In the next section we will talk more about other parts of developing a search strategy, but it helps greatly to develop your own systematic methods that work for you. Often, these methods will evolve from your own experience using a database. They often transfer to other databases, but may need to be modified as you do so. Good search strategy and systematic procedures will serve you well, however, in any database, and your research will benefit from precision and a comprehensive approach.

Proximity Searches

In full-text databases (and as we will see with Internet Search Engines) the Boolean commands do not always result in relevant matches. This is because two ANDed terms may occur in widely different parts of the document. A search for "gun control" and "legislation" may return a document that mentions gun control in the first paragraph and much later discusses drug legislation — the terms are completely unrelated in the document and yet the search retrieved the document. To more closely ally search terms, some databases employ a "proximity" connector. One possible example:

gun control W/5 legislation

This query stipulates that the phrase "gun control" must occur within five words of the term "legislation," effectively increasing the probability that the found match will likely be in the same sentence, or at least be closely related conceptually. The proximity connectors are particularly useful when a phrase search will not work. This problem often occurs in some names, as former U.S. President Bill Clinton's spouse now a senator can often be called Hilary Rodham Clinton or Hilary Clinton in the media. The search "Hilary w/3 Clinton" insures that all variants of the name will be retrieved, whereas a search merely for "Hilary Clinton" would come up empty some percentage of the time.

Limiting a Search

The power of computers to manipulate data allows for very specific instructions to be given when you want to make sense of that data. If a database of full-text articles from magazines contains 10 million articles, the odds are that you would not want to start with article number one and work your way through while you find related information. Computers allow you to be very specific in your requests for information.

One of these refining methods is called "limiting" which allows you to circumscribe your search results by a particular factor. You already do a little bit of this by using Boolean operators, limiting your results to a particular arrangement of keywords. However, databases allow for much greater precision.

Field limiting uses the arrangement of the database to refine your search. As mentioned earlier, databases are composed of records. Each record has a set of fields, and each record in the database has the same fields. As you go through the research process, you may begin with a research question similar to this:

> How is the Internet being used in schools to enhance the education of students?

However, as you progress, your research question may evolve:

How is the Internet being used in universities to enhance and enable the distance-learning opportunities for students?

You may realize that the Internet is a relatively recent introduction in the distance-learning programs of colleges and universities. Therefore, you would not be interested in research materials published before 1990. You could then limit your search to materials published only after 1990. The methods for doing this will vary from database to database, but generally speaking, if the publication date is part of a record, it is searchable. Your search statement may look something like this:

internet and universit? and distance-learning and py>1990

The code "py" represents "Publication Year" in some databases. Other databases may use other codes.

You may have to do several searches in one database to refine your search. As you view records and accept or reject them, you should pay attention to the fields in those records and investigate the possibility of searching by them. Fields such as authors, titles, institutions, subjects, dates, document types, could all be searchable, increasing your ability to retrieve exactly what you want out of a database.

In summary, the following tips are important to remember:

• Have some awareness of the database you are working with.

• The database determines the kinds of keywords you might use. In a specialized one like ERIC (a database devoted to education), using the words "education" or "learning" will not be very productive because nearly every record will have one of those words included in it somewhere.

• Be creative.

• Synonyms are often useful. If your first search is unproductive, do not give up but try to phrase the search in different terms.

• Modify as many times as necessary.

• Use field searches.

• If possible (not always in some databases) submit a word to the appropriate field. If you are looking for works written by Joyce Carol Oates, submit her name to an author field, which will then retrieve only records with her name as author and not works about her.

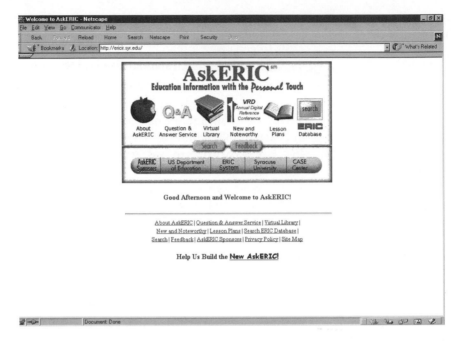

ERIC homepage *http://ericir.syr.edu/.* (ERIC Clearinghouse on Information and
Technology, National Library of Education, U.S. Dept. of Education. Courtesy
of the ERIC System.)

• Keep track of unusual or nonintuitive commands.

• Keep notes, use online help, and do whatever it takes to make your search-
    ing procedure smooth and effective.

Search Strategy

   One of the main challenges for researchers using electronic databases
involves the development of a useful search strategy. Knowing database
structure is helpful but will not in itself lead you to the information you
need. We have briefly looked at choosing search terms, which is a skill that
is developed over time. An old saying for computer programmers is "garbage in, garbage out," meaning that sloppy input guarantees sloppy output. In online searching, careless or imprecise search terms will often
deliver disappointing results. Besides search terms, however, are a number
of other factors for a successful search strategy. These include good choice
of database, evaluation of results, ability to modify searches depending on
results, and intuition to branch search into other fruitful areas.

Search Terms

The use of search terms to construct a search is essential to a search strategy. We have noted the differences between standardized search terms, such as the Library of Congress subject headings, and natural language search terms. Two parts of a successful choice of search terms are present: your own ability to define your topic or area and the use of the most precise terms possible when conducting a search. These qualities are occasionally at odds, and sometimes a balancing act is required. When conducting a search through a Web search engine, where a huge array of material is used as the database, precision becomes particularly important because choice of database is not an issue.

The choice of a topic is one you should already have made. You must have at least a preliminary idea of where your interests lie, and you then must attempt to distill one or more key concepts from that topic. One strategy for skimming keyword terms is to write a sentence about your topic, and then look for the most important nouns. Thus you might write, "I want to know more about the role played by semiotics in language." The main concepts involved in this sentence are "semiotics" and "language." The keywords are usually nouns (sometimes adjectives) stripped of all nonessential words, and your task as an online searcher is to construct a search that reflects these concepts.

Follow along as we examine some of the stages of online research.

Choice of Database

If your search is to be run on one of the Web search engines, choice of database can be irrelevant. If your search is to be made on a journal index, choice of database can be crucial. Having fabulously precise search terms will yield no benefit if the search is conducted in a database inappropriate for the search. The sample search on "language and semiotics" run in a medical database would be of absolutely no use.

The database chosen often depends greatly on the level of research required. Colleges and universities usually are well stocked with fairly specific databases that divide academic interests into extremely narrow but extremely comprehensive areas. For broader or less in-depth research, other databases may be more useful. The CARL UnCover index covers a wide range of academic journals and may be reached by a Web browser at http://uncweb.carl.org/. The federal government makes some databases available for public searching, notably the ERIC database for educational resources, which is one we will use for this sample search. (Although we were already familiar with the location of this resource, we could have arrived at the same place by using a Web index like Yahoo! and following the links to education and databases.)

Availability of databases for public use obviously has a lot to do with money. Some libraries are able to make databases available to their own users by virtue of their contract with the vendor or publisher of the database. Databases do not happen automatically. They are created by people and computers working at the myriad problems of indexing information, and consequently they have a market value. No one likes to see his or her hard work given away, unless that is the mandate from either a federal or other grant source. Thus accessibility will depend on your own situation and relationship to an educational institution or other organization. The national trend has been toward increasing availability of databases, and as payment methods can be devised, the trend will continue. Some databases, like CARL UnCover, are in the document delivery business, and they make their living delivering articles for a price but still provide a free indexing service to potential customers. Although database availability is in flux, we have tried to list solid addresses in the appendices, and the use of a Web index will also provide useful database addresses.

For our sample search we went to http://ericir.syr.edu/Eric/ where a search menu prompted us for our search terms, which we entered as "semiotics" and "language."

Evaluation of Results

Rarely will the first search ultimately deliver the best results. An initial search is often exploratory, and although even a preliminary search is improved if one gives thought to creating good search terms, some modification is often necessary.

The first search we used in the ERIC database was "semiotics" and "language." One clue to search success, but hardly the only one, is the number of records retrieved. One example mentioned earlier is a search in a library catalog using the search terms "civil war." Huge numbers of records are retrieved, but the researcher must then find ways to pinpoint a particular area or aspect of the topic in question. Another very common result is that apparently no records are retrieved — your carefully chosen search terms find no matches at all. There are several explanations for this result. Often the terms you applied in your search are not the terms used to index the material in the database. As mentioned before, highly specialized databases will use standardized indexing terms. If this possibility is present, the procedure should be to consult a thesaurus or to try other search terms that might be more likely to fit the discipline's grid of standardized terms.

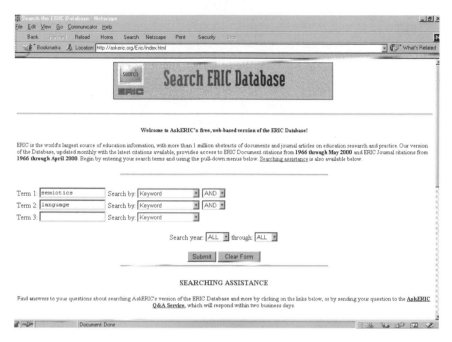

Search on ERIC for articles on the topic of semiotics in language. (ERIC Clearinghouse on Information and Technology, National Library of Education, U.S. Dept. of Education. Courtesy of the ERIC System.)

What could we do to make a more precise search, giving us a chance to see how this area has been researched? We realized that the best articles all had the keyword "semiotics" in the descriptor field. "Language" is a broad term that covers a lot of ground, while "semiotics" has a precise meaning for an indexer. So we modified our search and chose to use "semiotics" solely as a descriptor term, which combined with "language" as a more general keyword, improved our results. More of the articles had to do with our interest in the role of semiotics in language.

Another possible explanation for poor results has to do with the choice of database. Are you in the right place? There is always the chance that this particular interest of yours has not been researched to any great degree. Perhaps there is not much material at all. Maybe this is your chance to contribute to the world's understanding.

When dealing with large numbers of results, however, one finds that the choices often differ. Use of a thesaurus may help you see how your interest can be placed into a better category. Occasionally results may lead to another choice of search terms that more accurately reflect your interest but that you were unable to derive in your first attempt. Often in well-organized databases, it is possible to link, or jump, to different search terms that appear in your results.

Approaching your topic from an entirely different direction is occasionally useful as well. Perhaps you are in a database that handles your interest area extensively. Is there a different way to think about your topic? What else characterizes your interest? Of particular importance in modifying searches that retrieved large numbers of records is to add unusual or extremely precise terms, to winnow the field down to a manageable (and hopefully more carefully delineated) size. Sheer numbers of records should not in themselves force you to describe your interest more carefully. Perhaps there is just a lot of material on the topic.

Ability to Modify Search Depending on Evaluation

This usually involves a change of search terms, perhaps adding another term or limiting (or broadening) the set in some way. Problems can include either a paucity or a surplus of material, and we have spoken of how to

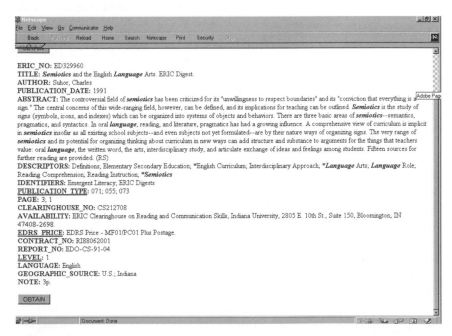

ERIC document citation with clearly labeled fields. (ERIC Clearinghouse on Information and Technology, National Library of Education, U.S. Dept. of Education. Courtesy of the ERIC System.)

expand or limit your searches. Remember that the Boolean connector "AND" will decrease the size of sets because all records must include both combined terms, whereas the "OR" connector will broaden sets, invoking documents with either of the terms. The "NOT" term is particularly useful when you need to weed a category out, as in the 1996 U.S. presidential race: the search "DOLE NOT PINEAPPLE" eliminates all the extraneous articles dealing with the Dole pineapple company rather than the Republican candidate.

This phase of the search takes some practice, and it is not always immediately apparent how to change a search to get better results. Much trial and error is involved for even the best searchers, but when alternative terms and careful combining have already proved unsuccessful, any sort of creativity you may choose to use may prove helpful.

Branching or Chaining

If your search retrieves even a small number of good records or documents, try to discover how they were indexed or how they showed up in your set. What else about them brought them to the surface? What other terms did they contain that you might use for an additional search? Perhaps it is worth looking for other work by the same person, who may have done related studies but with a different focus and title. One of the standard features of most document retrieval search engines is that although they may not always deliver well in the first instance, if you can discover useful documents, it is much easier to then craft a search that will retrieve similar documents.

In this case we found a good selection of journal articles, some of them more appropriate to our interest than others. In looking at the records, which are extremely well indexed, we noticed that certain terms kept appearing in the "descriptor" field, meaning that the indexers had applied that term to the article, thus grouping it with other articles of similar content. The ERIC database, like many well-organized databases, allows you to specify what field your term can be applied to, and we chose to make it a "descriptor" term in the hopes of retrieving more relevant material. In fact, this proved useful and made for a more tightly defined set of articles.

In traditional research an analogous practice is sometimes called "footnote chasing." When something good shows up, it is worth checking all the footnotes given in the article. If the research is good, the material the author picked is probably also worth examining, and following up promising leads may bring you to surprisingly good resources.

Internet Search Services

Internet search services include a variety of locating tools that attempt to improve your ability to find Internet information. One of the great criticisms of the Internet is that it is not organized and that the wealth of information it offers cannot be easily discovered. The searching mechanisms address this very real need by the use of increasingly sophisticated information retrieval technology and often permit discovery of valuable material for research from locations that are not intuitively obvious.

There are two types of Internet Search Services, but rarely do examples of either type exist in a pure form. Instead, most are hybrids, combining elements of both. One kind is an index of material, and the best example of this type is Yahoo! (others include Magellan, Galaxy, and the CERN Virtual Library). The second type involves the use of word searches done by search engines that find documents with keywords that match those submitted as query terms. This second kind has several examples, notably AltaVista, Google, and many others. Each type has advantages.

Internet Indexes

Indexes arrange their lists of URLs in a hierarchy. In practice they have analogs in the library and archive world in that there is a classification scheme employed to group similar kinds of information resources together. Although the classification employed by Internet indexes is nowhere nearly as rigorous or comprehensive as that in a library, partly due to the extreme fluidity and diversity of electronic resources in general, it enables a researcher to scan a list of potential categories before deciding where to begin looking for information.

Although indexes are at best imperfect representations of how we (or at least those of us who spend our time classifying things) group categories of knowledge, they often provide an excellent starting point for research. Particularly when you do not have a clear idea of a topic or research question and only have a vague sense of your interests, browsing through an index can be a delightful way to provoke ideas. For a real-world comparison, suppose I need some household hardware of some sort to perform a repair; I may not always know exactly what is necessary to do the job. I may have a broken part, which I can diligently carry to a hardware store to try to match. Luckily, most hardware stores are fairly well organized and have an assortment of aisles, some with plumbing supplies, others with nails and other fasteners, and others with rope, twine, and other materials for tying things together. Proceeding by general category (in this case usually according to purpose —

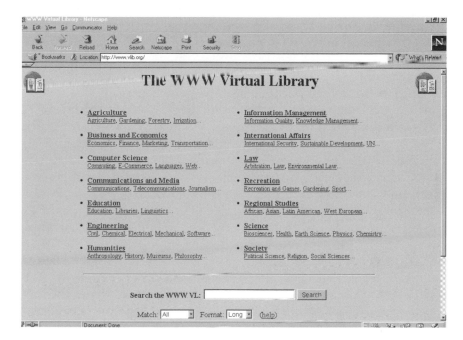

World Wide Web Virtual Library *http://vlib.org.* (Image courtesy of the WWW Virtual Library.)

electrical, plumbing, woodworking, etc.), I can go to approximately the right place and browse the shelves for items that may fit my repair need. I can examine the materials, think over their potential utility, and make my choice.

Indexes like Yahoo! simplify the looking part of the process. Similar resources are grouped together. I may not agree with how the resources have been divided up, but the scheme is consistent, and I do not have to think too hard to realize that my interest in photography will probably come under the heading of "Arts." (Depending on my level of interest, I could also look for photography resources in the Recreation category and, in fact, would find a section there that would bring me to the same group of listings appearing in the "Arts-Photography" section, an example of cross listing.)

Indexes are also particularly valuable when you are unsure of correct terminology for a topic. Seeing a list can often prompt you to think of your topic in a new and useful light. In cases where your topic is extremely narrowly focused and you have not been able to uncover much material about it, seeing a classification can often help you move "up" or "down" one level of category into a broader or narrower treatment of your topic. While rummaging in the "Arts" category looking for "Photography," I may find another subcategory, perhaps "Computer Generated," that seems promising but that had not occurred to me earlier. Although the categories themselves sometimes present problems (some topics could be placed under a variety of headings, for example), they serve to place things with similar attributes in the same bin.

Indexes like Yahoo! will often offer a searching mechanism as well, to browse through their list of lists, but one of the characteristics of indexes is the human component of categorization. Although computers are capable of rapid and sophisticated pattern matches, they do not perform as well as human minds for creating classes of things. Nor should they be. Categories themselves are artificial constructs in that we, as thinking beings, have created them. Computers, at their current level of technology, cannot mirror certain kinds of human thinking, but a good index will follow, as much as possible, the natural ways that humans think about their world and interests.

There is no perfect index anywhere in the world because of the different ways that people think about knowledge and the universe of things. The best indexes are ones that reflect their users' interests and concerns, and various specialty disciplines often have well-organized, highly useful indexes of material. This is generally because the creators of the indexes have a good idea of what users will want when they employ the index. But for the entire human community, not all needs are identical, and thinking often proceeds according to need. Even library systems of long duration are not in perfect agreement on classification, which is another piece of evidence to support theories of diversity of categorization. But the Internet benefits from attempts to organize its wealth of material, and Web indexes are valuable research tools.

Search Engines

The mechanisms employed by various companies to ferret out documents on the Net have traditionally been called "search engines," a term lifted from the Information Retrieval field of study. In operation they are all pieces of software with very simple goals, and are all similar to each other in their basic functioning. They take keyword query terms, supplied by the searcher, and look for matches amongst their compilations of index tables that the system has created over time. These tables are created by automated software applications sometimes called "spiders" or "crawlers" (obviously referring to the imagery generated by the name of the World Wide Web). The search engines return a set of results, often ranked according to a formula designed to deliver superior results first, and appear to be very similar in operation to the search mechanisms employed by structured databases.

As noted earlier, the ways that computers locate relevant material have both strengths and weaknesses. One powerful improvement over traditional human methods is that they can quickly cover enormous amounts of material. A keyword phrase can be noted in thousands of records in a split second. Complex searches with a variety of attributes (or facets) can produce results of astonishing precision. Conversely, computer searches are quite capable of retrieving records that have nothing to do with the interest of the researcher but merely result from a word match. The inherent ambiguity of the English language, which allows different meanings to be assigned to the same word, contributes to this seemingly illogical result.

Returning to the hardware store analogy, if I went to the store in search of some screws for my household project and employed an automatic robot instead of using my native cunning to browse the (well-arranged) aisles, the robot could conceivably return (after perusing the entire store) with everything that had a screw in it somewhere. The set of things would be a wildly disparate collection. It would include all sorts of boxes of screws, some of them maybe even the kind I was looking for, but also a wide array of other material, much of it of no use for my project. There might be birdhouses of wood held together with screws, tools assembled with screws, a rake with a screw fastening its handle to its prongs. The robot would have done its job properly. It had been given something to match, in this case a screw, and it went out and did its work efficiently and thoroughly, although without intelligence.

In order to be satisfied with the robotic service (and such systems, also called "bots," are at work in the Internet), I need to know what to ask for and how to phrase my request to maximize the chances of getting something that resembles what I really want. If I want a box of screws but no brass wood screws, I need to ask specifically in that way. The skills associated with framing a search outlined in our electronic searching section are essential to make use of the searching mechanisms found for the World Wide Web. Sometimes I can also maximize the usefulness of my set by sending the robot out into only one section of the store. This helps avoid mismatches and may also save time because the searching range has been circumscribed.

These search engines are similar in operation and employ automated searching mechanisms that use keywords entered by the user to find matches in the documents in the search engines range. The major differences arise in the amount of the Web that the search engines cover, how quickly and how thoroughly they update their field, and what parts of the documents they use for searching. Trade-offs abound, obviously. As we will see, some search engines include more material than others, which makes a difference in the results. Some of the automatic search engines update their range fairly frequently and are constantly adding new sites or other new additions. All of them look in document titles and body text for matches, but some do "deeper" indexing than others. The way URLs are counted also makes a difference, and some of the search engines will not count a URL unless it is a usable one, whereas others just count occurrences of the URLs.

It is tempting to think that looking through all parts of a document must be preferable, but because title or abstract searching may leave out your particular interest, the length of time required for the search obviously increases.

These search engines, as well as the indexes, are "free" in the sense that they do not charge any fee for someone to use them. They are generally not charitable organizations, however, and must pay for their staff time and computing resources. This leads to a variety of means of producing revenue, which can include displaying advertising and charging a fee to those organizations that wish to be listed in their directories. Some, like public broadcasting media, have paid sponsors. Often a main aim of the company is to sell its searching services and other Web-based or computer applications to other companies. Thus the search engine is a free opportunity for the company's expertise to be tested and explored.

Search terms may be combined differently with the different search engines. For example Lycos automatically uses an understood Boolean "AND" between search terms, but WebCrawler utilizes explicit Boolean commands.

Some of the Web search engines utilized WAIS (Wide Area Information Service) search mechanisms, which can be recognized by their distinctive weighted display of resources. One annoying aspect of Web search engines is brought out when a Web page designer puts a large number of words into the document purposely to make for a skewed retrieval.

Although the automated nature of many search engines may make them seem relatively simple to develop, the complexities of good search mechanisms are legion. A few special search engines available in commercial applications improve on word-matching abilities (by giving extra "weight" to a keyword found in a title or abstract, as opposed to the body of the text), but there are some unavoidable problems in current search engines. For this reason it often is best to combine the use of an index with the use of a search engine when looking for resources.

Much of the development work on information retrieval was done some time ago, and there are theoretical models that address many of the shortcomings of current search engines, but implementation has met formidable obstacles. With the rapid growth of the use of the Web, search

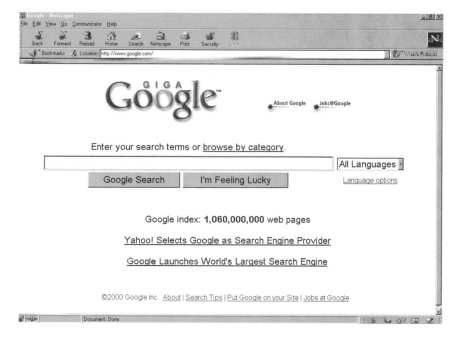

Google *http://www.google.com.* (Copyright © 2000 Google Inc.)

engines have an opportunity for extensive development. Economic factors will probably motivate such development.

Many commercial services have economic interests in providing software and hardware for companies doing business and other organizations. Much work on intranets, which are mini-internets within a given organization, has been done recently, and many organizations are looking for good ways to disseminate internal information to all their members. Security of the information is just one of the many problem areas for this sort of endeavor, and many search services have grappled with these and a variety of other issues. Netscape's Navigator and Microsoft's Internet Explorer have battled for dominance in the browser wars, each of them claiming unique features. Everyone wants a piece of the huge and growing Internet-wealth pie, and the battles for position (and dominance) are fierce. With luck, the Internet user will benefit, as improvements in search engines become more widespread, but economic battles over market share have not always been a boon in the long haul for consumers.

Search Engine Operation

These Internet search engines differ from their database counterparts however, and it may be useful to examine some of the aspects of these differences.

The first and perhaps most major difference lies in the differences of the records each system is looking for. Databases have very structured records, with well-organized fields for author, title, subject, date, etc. Internet documents on the other hand, mostly have only the barest outline of organization. Most Webpages will have a title, a clearly helpful attribute, not only for search engines but as a means of identifying important data about the page. But only if an author has been unusually conscientious will his or her Webpage list authorship, or date, or other information known as "metadata"— information about information — in the document's structure. We will look more fully at this issue in a moment, but for now it is enough to recognize that this difference between database and internet search engines explains a great deal about their potential success when successful results for a query are desired.

Besides the issues of metadata, there are differences due to the nature of the documents themselves. Internet search engines often operate in a manner more similar to full-text search engines, since both are often looking at matches within a fairly large field of text. Bibliographic records, on the other hand, are usually quite short, with a set of clearly delineated fields. Often only a handful of these fields are searchable (author, title, subject terms, abstract) and so the keyword matches are apt to be more precise. But in full-text databases, the search terms used can often be found in many different parts of the documents retrieved. The Boolean AND becomes much weaker here, since ANDed terms in a document may be found miles apart and have no real relation. Phrase searching or proximity searching often are better bets.

Although database search engines will differ amongst themselves to some degree in the manner which they require search terms to be combined, the Internet search engines show even greater variation. Unfortunately and even worse, the Internet search engines do not even always make it clear how they treat query strings, whether the terms are automatically "ANDed" together or "ORed"— a huge difference with respect to results. For example, Fast Search www.alltheweb.com uses an automatic AND, while Excite http://excite.com/search uses a default OR. Some want a plus sign "+" if the term is required (no documents without that term will be retrieved) and others like to have quotation marks around a phrase. If you do not know some of these details, your searches can easily be unsatisfying.

The requirements are usually included in the help screens or online explanations, but are not often immediately obvious. Some search engines can handle complex boolean queries, others make use of only fairly simple search strings. Probably one of the best ways to compare this aspect of the different search engine behaviors is to look at one of the many comparison charts that exist. Walt Howe and Hope Tillman have compiled a good chart at http://www0.delphi.com/navnet/faq/searchcomparison.html and another useful one by Carole Leita is at http:www.infopeople.org/src/chart.html. These charts are helpful for quick comparisons, as well as highlighting the standardization problems of this arena of internet life.

The standardization of terminology is also an issue. Most databases employ some version of what is called "controlled vocabulary," or a list of commonly accepted terms, to provide a foundation for their subject headings. Internet documents rarely adhere to any standard of categorization. Even when an author has supplied his document with keyword "metatags" (more on these in a moment) they are self-derived and may not conform to any accepted standard.

The final main difference between database and Internet search engines has to do with the size of the collection of items being sifted. In a database, there is a finite set of documents, and a given index may belimited to a certain set of journals that it tracks, perhaps only those ones judged the most important one of the field. Thus even a fairly large index like Carl UnCover at http://uncweb.carl.org is handling only the contents of a limited set — some 17,000 journals. The Internet however, while not yet on the horizon of infinity, is ever growing, morphing its contents, and shifting its addresses. It also possesses a formidable size — far larger than the contents of 17,000 journals over a period of many years. Size is a major difference.

What the Internet search engines do to find their matches is of some interest too. Their "spiders" or "search and index" mechanisms compile lists of index tables, which the search engines then employ for use when a searcher submits a query. Rather than apparently sending your search to Fast Search for "civil war" out to 340 million Webpages separately and simultaneously (wherein it claims "785361 documents found" in "0.1256 seconds search time"— how impressive!) it is matched against a much smaller number of index tables which then deliver a list of URLs which fit the bill. This economical mechanism allows the apparent speed of the search engine.

So immediately one of the questions that emerges when considering a search engine is "how much of the Web does the engine's 'crawler' index?" and further "how often does it update its index tables?"

Bragging rights for the largest amount of the Internet that is indexed has flopped from search engine to search engine as time and technological evolution progress. As of July 2000, some engines claim indexes of over 500 million Webpages, although there is reason to think the numbers are inflated. One independent survey by Carole Leita ©2000 InFoPeople Project, (http://www.infopeople.org/src/guide.html) lists a range of coverage from 560 million pages (Google) to second place Alta Vista and Fast Search at 340 million.

Other Search Engine Quirks

A few search engines employ a measure called link popularity to rank their results sets. This measure makes the assumption that if Dr. Joan Ralston's Website on Headaches is "pointed to" by more other Websites than Frank Bemesten's similar site, then it should be given a higher relevance ranking in the returned lists of URLs. Google in particular takes this mechanism a step further, and gives weight to the location of the "pointer site." Thus a link from a prestigious university Website is assumed to have better quality than a link from http://commercial-sleeze.com, and will boost the score of the linked-to page. This assumption is an optimistic view of the leveling factor of numbers and the Web community, which has some controversial elements to it. Is a popularity count always a measure of excellence? Probably not all the time, but the empirical results from sites like Google that employ this device are often superior to other search engines.

Other search engines, notably Northern Light, make human qualities of discrimination a part of this service. When a search is submitted to Norther Light, the results are grouped into "folders" organized by type, subject, language, etc. This process, somewhat similar to that employed by some library catalogs (although much easier to do there, where the records are so much more standardized and well structured), allows the searcher to browse different facets of the search results and helps focus in on particular aspects of the topic for further study. Human intervention obviously is at work at various Indexes like Yahoo! or the WWW Virtual Library, which utilize subject divisions to organize their information.

In fact it is not so easy to accurately count the amount of material covered — do you count all the pages at one site that are in your index, do you include "deep indexing" which some engines use to catalog pages that are not directly counted, but instead are suggested by their "links to" URLs, and do you include pages only superficially indexed (document title only perhaps?)? There are duplicate documents too, the same file posted at more than one site — how do you treat these? Many of the engines utilize indexes of over 200 million pages at this stage, and as the Web grows, so will these

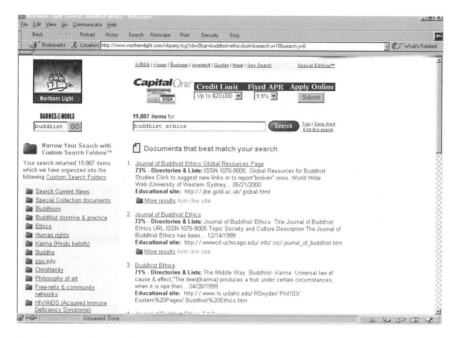

Northern Light Results in a search for "Buddhist Ethics" *http://www.northern-light.com/.* **(Printed with permission of Northern Light Technology, Inc.)**

indexes. From the searcher's perspective, bigger is not always better, however, especially if quality is the desired attribute in a document.

Practical Searching

At the early stages of a project, it makes sense to employ both indexes and search engines. As you accumulate material, modifications to your research interests are almost inevitable, and with luck some of the resources uncovered will point to other useful resources as well.

The same techniques we mentioned for the beginning of any research project hold especially true for research employing the Web: define your topic, phrase your question, distill potentially useful search terms, and be prepared to modify your searches as you go along, depending on your evaluation of the material discovered.

Generally, a well-designed index is relatively straightforward to use: a series of categories is displayed at the initial page of the site, and one merely selects the most appropriate categories to browse. Subcategories often are displayed under the initial, fairly broad, categories, and the choices are a mouse-click away. Good indexes maintain a series of useful (up-to-date and consequently active) URL links. You can often tell when you have pretty well exhausted a subject area when all the sites begin to refer to each other.

The worst thing that can happen with an index is that there does not appear to be any category that covers your own interest. The only real options open to you are to employ a search engine, hoping that your highly focused topic can be found that way, or to determine a broader category that your interest might fit under.

The use of search engines is also fairly straightforward. The main screen of the service has a dialog box where you may type your search terms. Some, like AltaVista, give you a choice of what kinds of searches you may wish to employ (with options for simple and advanced searches). Some of the hybrid search services have different categories, similar to index categories, in which to submit a search. These smaller subranges save searching time and often improve the relevance of retrieved documents.

One common mistake is to assume that the number of records returned from the search has any correlation to utility. Not all sets will be tidy and limited. Of greater importance is the percentage of relevant material retrieved, which could occur in large or small sets of records. Many search engines only return a limited number of records anyway, but you should be aware that this number does not equal efficiency. Some search engines will return a greater percentage of useful material depending on their range or the flexibility of their search mechanism itself.

Search Engine Tips

When conducting a search using an Internet Search engine, a few habits will increase your success in getting quality information, some of them identical or similar to the principles used for success in databases.

Unusual words — the more unusual the term you employ, the less likely it will be to match irrelevant material. A more precise, less ambiguous term is always better than a common one.

More words is invariably better than fewer — additional words generally serve to flesh out a topic by including facets of the topic that you are interested in, for better results. Thus "civil war + transportation + economics + railroad" as a query serves to capture several different attributes of your interest. Be aware of how your chosen search engine deals with multiple terms (the plus sign for most of them means that term must be included in a match, but systems vary in their syntax requirements).

Take advantage of feedback mechanisms — many engines have developed ways of helping you home in on your interest. Northern Light, for example, gives you a list of folders after submitting your query which can help you select the area that seems most appropriate for your study. Other systems may have a link for "related sites" (Alta Vista) "find similar sites" (Go) or the like, that allow you to find sites that might not normally have appeared with your first search. These may use different terms or be indexed in a way that was not obvious to you.

Use fields if possible — if your first search provides thousands of pages, perhaps due to the popularity of the topic, perhaps try a search in only the title field, which often improves the chances that your document is strongly "about" your chosen topic keyword.

Limit — again using fields, you may want to limit to an "edu" domain for example if you do not want any commercial sites to be included (alternatively you can use the NOT connector or otherwise use an exclude mechanism for any domain that includes ".com." This feature is often only available in search engines' "advanced mode." You may want to limit by language or date (particularly if currency is important) or some other attribute to winnow down your list of results.

Use an index — Yahoo! at http://www.yahoo.com/, the WWW Virtual Library at http://vlib.org/ or some other index like the Librarian's Index may provide you with a better organized starting place for your search, where you can pick categories and more productively browse material.

Get help — there are lots of books and other online guides at this stage that serve to help you identify good resources. Check the extensive bibliography at the end of this work for books that may serve to cover your topic area so that you can take advantage of someone else's footwork.

Another perhaps greater drawback to document retrieval on the Web is the sometimes ambiguous way that documents are indexed. The frequent use of a particular word in a document may bring it to the forefront of a search, regardless of whether the word is properly used or whether the document has anything to do with the topic. Some documents are deliberately falsely tagged, perhaps loaded up with a handful of nonrelated words at their tail end, or even hidden in nondisplayed text (HTML documents often have text that is not displayed with a browser but exists to identify authorship or other aspects of the document). Searching mechanisms are always looking for new sites, URLs to add to their range of material, and those with Web pages are solicited to add their sites to the search database. The owner of the site may do a good job of describing the Web site, employing useful descriptive terms, or the site may be described in a careless or (unintentionally) misleading way. The search service has no control over the indexing terms provided by the site owner. It merely adds the record to its list of URLs, and the search results using such a list are not always satisfactory. Again the lack of standardization becomes a drawback.

Web Documents

Given the proliferation of information posted on the World Wide Web and the ease of publication, it may make some sense to consider how these documents are created and what characteristics are inherent in their creation that affect how they are found, the main interest of the researcher. Potential Web authors should look at the appendix on Web Page Creation for more discussion of some of these issues.

One of the beauties of the Web is how it evolved so that the dominant file is a plain text creation. As noted earlier, when it comes to transferring files over the Internet, there is a major difference between text (or ASCII files) and binary (everything else — images, sound, movie files). Web documents, although often loaded with graphics and images, are plain text at their core (or in their framework, if you will), and so can be edited in a word processor or even the simple text editors that come with most operating systems (teachtext in Macintosh, Notepad in windows, or Unix-based editors like *pico.*) This increases their flexibility to those who would create them.

Web documents use HTML, a so-called markup language, an outgrowth of SGML, which is still used for many full-text document collections. As a markup language, it is quite different from a programming language like C++ or Visual Basic. It is easy enough to apply the basic HTML tags to a document and upload it to a Webserver in order to make it available to the rest of the world using a browser. (Some Web aficionados might claim that it is too easy.)

In the simplest Web document, there is a body of text that is marked to be viewed by a browser. The document's title is represented by a field tag and its heading by another.

```
<HTML>
<HEAD>
<TITLE>Title</TITLE>
                            </HEAD>
<BODY>
        Text
                            </BODY>
</HTML>
```

The tags are just markers, that tell the browser what to do when confronted with a document, and most tags must be activated ("turned on" like a light switch) with a command such as <BOLD> and then "turned off" after that function is through with a command with a backslash, </BOLD>.

Non-text information (pictures, sound) are included by putting "pointers" in the HTML text that tell the browser to find another file at the Website. The browser does this automatically, and depending on the speed of your Internet connection, seamlessly (big graphic files are notoriously difficult to load over slower dialup connections.) Increasingly most Websites, especially big commercial sites, are apt to be packed to bursting with lots of extra non-text files, all attached to the file you have called up on your browser.

Each tag tells the browser what to do with the information, so common tags are for title, bold or italic for how words will be displayed, formatting tags, and all the other fancy formatting that goes on — tables, frames, headers, etc.

All this matters sometimes when considering search engine behavior. Where is the engine looking for matches? Just titles and body text? Or is it looking in attached files as well (where choice of a file name makes a big difference)? Metatags are a whole different issue, and the reality of their uncertain reliability as an indicator of quality is measured by the number of search engines that deliberately ignore them (Google, Northern Light and Lycos, among others).

Metadata

Metadata is information about information, or more accurately, the kinds of bibliographic information usually considered vital by librarian types: author, title, date of publication. Current metatags on Web documents often also include information about the language and character set with which the document is composed.

A well designed Webpage will include two especially useful metatags: description and keywords. Thus a Website on cognitive philosophy might include these metatags:

```
<Html>
<Title> Cognitive Science Resources </Title>
<META NAME="title" content="Cognitive Science Resources: Internet
  sites">
<META NAME="author" content="N. Fielden, San Francisco State Uni-
  versity">
<META NAME="description" content="Links to the electronic sites
  devoted to Cognitive Science around the Internet.">
```

```
<META NAME="keywords" content="cognitive science, mind, con-
sciousness, empirical philosophy, cognitive philosophy, Internet
resources">
```

The description tag describes the document in question in unambiguous terms. The keyword tag includes descriptive terms, keywords and
other synonyms of concept terms that are connected with the document's
topic. Many search engines will use these terms when composing their
index tables, since, after all, the author of the page has seen fit to use these
terms to describe the document in question. In some way, they might be
compared to an abstract field on a record for a journal article, yet their
shortcomings are obvious. First, they are author composed. Authors often
are not the best persons to catalog a given document — the topic is too close
to their heart for a good broad view categorization. Second, these terms
may not be standardized the way a good library catalog or database would
operate. Third, and perhaps most importantly, they lead to the deceptive
practices of some commercially driven sites.

Metatags for the Webpage on Buddhist Ethics, with good descriptive
text in the name and keyword fields look like this:

```
<meta name="description" content="Buddhist ethics is concerned with
the principles and practices that help one to act in ways that help
rather than harm. The core ethical code of Buddhism is known as the
five precepts.">
<meta name="keywords" content="Buddhism, Buddhist, ethics, prin-
ciples, skilful, unskilful, precepts, loving kindness, metta, generosity,
contentment, truthfulness, mindfulness, morality">
```

Commercial Interests and Spamming

All of this locating business is also compromised by the restless, raging desire of many Website designers who want to catch your attention
and have their site noticed by a search engine. This desire results in all sorts
of tricks by Webpage designers. Ambiguous (even deceptive) meta keywords are used, hidden text, huge numbers of keywords packed into the
document, all manner of deceit.

The notion of "spam," unwelcome commercial email solicitations, has
been extended to the Web since the first edition of this book appeared.
Spamming is now a term applied to Websites that deliberately attempt to
mislead a search engine into giving them greater notice than they deserve.
This is the biggest headache for most current search engine designers, who

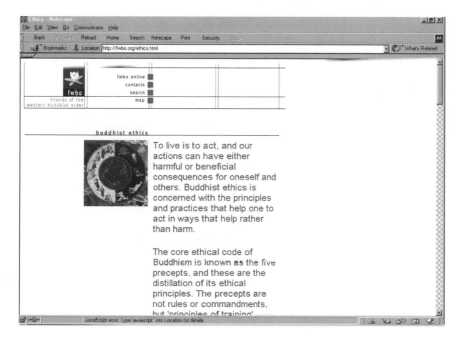

Friends of the Western Buddhist Order Ethics Page, *http://fwbo.org/ethics.html*. (Reprinted with permission of fwbo.)

work hard to develop locating algorithms that find quality documents, only to have their result sets ruined by the spamming practices of other Websites.

For many Web marketers, getting their "foot in your door" (the current Internet marketing jargon for this is "grabbing eyeballs") is worth considerable effort, and the spammers are not above all kinds of activity that crosses the borders of decency.

Some Web documents are crammed full of extra text, counting on the search engines tendency to reward sites with multiple terms a higher ranking than those with fewer. Normally if a student's class term paper (posted online at the course homepage) was titled "Gender and Race on the Web" and mentioned each of these terms dozens of times in its text, most search engines would give it a high index ranking for those topics. But spammers could create a document with the words, "gender, race, web" repeated over and over in the text, and their bogus site (maybe selling pornography or a get-rich-quick scheme) just might get a click from you, the unsuspecting researcher looking for material on this topic. Nine times out of ten, the visitor would pass on with a shrug of exasperation, but every once in awhile somebody would visit the site with attention and the spammer's goal has been reached.

Some documents have misleading keywords in their metatag field for keywords, others have keywords in "invisible" print (text in the same color as the document's background color)—which therefore do not appear on your browser's screen but which are noticed by the search engine. Other methods of "stuffing" a page with keywords involve the use of small font text, again barely noticeable on the document, but given unwanted weight by the search engine. Like many deceptive practices, spamming ends up being a cat and mouse game between search engine designers and the online marketers hoping to get a look from the increasingly large community of Internet citizens.

Some search engines ignore invisible or tiny text in the creation of their indexes, others like Google rely on the strength of their link popularity mechanisms to weed out unwanted material. But no method is foolproof, and this little battle is likely to proceed for some time.

Perhaps it is helpful at this stage to remember the recent origins of the Web. Books have been around for centuries, and in large numbers thanks to printing press technology that became widespread after the sixteenth century. Web documents, on the other hand, have a history of only a decade, and the ways that we think of them, organize them, categorize them, list them, sort them and find them, are very new. The process of designing standards for these documents, both in how they are created, and how they will be seen and understood, is an exercise in contortion and compromise for those engaged in it. Given the free-form independent streak of many Net citizens, this process may take a long time to settle down to a productive equilibrium.

5
Internet Subject Resources

This section provides general guidelines for conducting research using the Internet. Each of the subsections, arranged by broad subject category, contain more specific hints for research strategies, list important resources and outline some of the distinctions of the particular discipline.

To be comprehensive in your research, consult the bibliography, and utilize other works more carefully targeted for resources in your area of interest. Mostly only Internet sites with a fairly high degree of stability are listed, but this is always a problem, because the online environment changes so quickly. See my list at http://userwww.sfsu.edu/~fielden/internetresearch.htm for the most current and accurate list of Internet links from this book.

This introductory section lists suggestions that may pertain to all the other sections and should assist you in locating and utilizing Internet information. Many of the initial suggestions are extensions of your own common sense but are worth noting as you engage in the research process.

1. Stay Organized

Easy to say, hard to do. But organization of your process can save you time and make your efforts more useful. Do whatever it takes to document your progress and retain your ideas. You can keep a notebook next to your workstation, which is handy for jotting down ideas, the search terms you employed, connections between concepts, pathways that turned into dead ends, and those forays that look promising. You can alternatively keep a computer-based notebook. Open a file on your computer, either in a word-processing application or in a text editor (Simpletext for Macintosh or Notepad in Windows, or even a file in your own Internet account), and make your notes as you go along, copying down URL addresses or annotations to your efforts.

This method is extremely handy if you have cut-and-paste as an option in your operating system because you can quickly, and accurately, copy long addresses and other file information for safekeeping. You may want to use a combination method, where your actual notebook (which can have your handwritten efforts— the diagrams, arrows showing connections, and other effects hard to duplicate on your computer) can incorporate printouts from your computer files, perhaps even with a sleeve or protective enclosure for you to take a floppy disk along with you when you go foraging at a workstation other than your normal computer. Keeping careful track of your results can save you valuable time and effort in your hunting, and when it comes time to document your results, you will not need to run the search again to verify sources.

2. Be Flexible and Inventive

Research has a tendency to be nonlinear, and no matter how much we speak of methods and approaches, rarely does progress march perfectly straight down the field. Seldom are the first search terms the best ones. Be prepared to modify your searches (and your thinking), depending on the results of your retrievals. Continually try new directions, and do not be afraid to follow your instincts. What are the qualities that stand out most in your most useful retrievals? What kinds of branching queries can you think of that might lead to other fertile areas? Are you in the best database for your search? How might you limit the percentage of irrelevant "hits"?

This is the area of research that is difficult to systematize. Your intuition here is one of the intangible assets you bring to the discovery of information. Creativity in the world is not limited to performing arts, writing, and composing — it has a place in the research process. No computer can associate ideas as well as you, the researcher. You are able to find patterns, intuit movements, and divine frameworks from your data in an incomparable manner. Your use of computer technology can extend your abilities but cannot replace them.

Persistence is another attribute that assists your progress, and there is not a major discovery in the world that did not benefit from this essential ingredient.

3. Know Some Standard Strategies

• *Use an Index*— Yahoo! at http://www.yahoo.com/ and the World Wide Web Virtual Library at http://vlib.org/) offer collections of pages and links to a multitude of useful sites. Their organization of Internet resources does two major things for you. By arranging resources by major categories, they vastly improve your chances of finding relevant material, as well as saving you a good deal of time. While search engines are wonderful things, they are often quite capable of generating large lists of irrelevant material. The indexes have been compiled with thought and care by humans, and generally reflect useful subject divisions of information. The second advantage of this approach is that it gives you an idea of what is out there — what sorts of things are available and the general areas where the "good stuff" is located. This can frequently lead to "branching" inquiries, where you poke around related areas and often discover things you might not have initially considered.

Some other indexes include the Galaxy, a very broadly based index at http://galaxy.einet.net/galaxy.html and Magellan at http://magellan.excite.com/.

Increasingly there are specialized indexes as well, that often serve to further research interests better in their selective qualities of compilation. One favorite of librarians, which works very well for plenty of others as well, is the Librarian's Index at http://lii.org/.

- *Use Appropriate Search Terms* — This one takes practice, and we have looked in detail at some of the fine points of generating useful search terms in Chapter 4. When using a search engine, try to distill the most important aspects of your topic or question into concepts that can be represented in bite-sized keywords. If your results are not what you expected (or wanted), try refining your topic or describing it more precisely.

  Use alternative terms, perhaps synonyms of your original keywords. If feasible, consult a thesaurus for alternative terms. Many subject disciplines have specific lists of subjects, often peculiar to their own territory, that make for improved search terms. When you do find something useful, pay attention to the terminology used because those words might prove helpful in conducting another search.

- *Look in the Right Place* — This is another one that takes practice and makes for interesting initial headaches (how do I know where to look when I don't know where to begin?). Pick databases that reflect your major interest, or alternatively, start broadly and be prepared to narrow in on particular areas. The indexes mentioned earlier are invaluable for this approach. If using a search engine, familiarize yourself with the peculiarities of its operation, how it combines terms and the syntax it requires for successful searches. Does the search engine automatically "OR" terms together if no Boolean operators are specified? Does it require the use of any symbols or other combining mechanisms?

Librarians' Index to the Internet *http://lii.org/*. (©Copyright 2000 by Librarians' Index to the Internet.)

Reading the online help screens on a first visit is rarely a waste of your time.

- *Survey Some Databases*— A good broad-ranging, but scholarly, database is maintained by CARL UnCover in Colorado at http://uncweb.carl.org. They are in the business of document delivery (faxing hard copy reprints from journal articles to you, the consumer), but their index is free and gives you an excellent method of checking journals for articles dealing with your area of interest. Two of the best maintained by different arms of the U.S. government are ERIC for Education related materials and Grateful Med for Medical resources. Many other databases are proprietary, but check to see what else might be available to you.

- *Consider Newsgroups and Mailing Lists*— Refer to the session on these tools, but remember that finding appropriate ones for your topic can often be easily accomplished by using Kovac's http://www.n2h2.com/KOVACS/ or Liszt's http://www.liszt.com/ Websites, which maintain a list of lists and groups. These can put you in touch with others with similar interests, and can lead to resource sharing and cooperation in your efforts.

• *Subject Specialists on the Net*— One strategy, often startlingly successful, is to utilize the work of various University specialists who have created research guides for their areas. A good college or university site will often contain a number of highly relevant Website links, often found in the Library under the tile of Research Guides. While these guides are often oriented towards standard academic sources that either do not occur online or are limited to the campus community, there are often Websites listed of unusual quality. See for example guides from San Francisco State University at http://library.sfsu.edu/instruc-tion/guides/guides.html, Columbia at http://www.columbia.edu/cu/libraries/subjects/, and Smith College at http://www.smith.edu/libraries/subject/.

• *Respect Copyright and Other Intellectual Property Issues*— A lot available from the Internet is free and public, with no restrictions on usage. But much reflects the hard work of individuals or of groups of individuals who may want credit or financial remuneration for the use or reprint of their efforts. Regardless of your own personal feelings on this issue, you may run afoul of the law if you are careless or flagrant in the copy-ing, distributing, or use without authorization of various materials. Be careful and respectful, and the Internet will serve us all.

• *Share Your Results!*— If you have found something really special, tell oth-ers about it. Whether it is something you have discovered or a conclu-sion you have reached from your own research, it may have more value if others can benefit from it. You can do this in a number of ways: com-municating (in any format) with friends and others, posting to news-groups or mailing lists, or putting it on your own Web page. But wealth deserves to be spread around, and one of the Internet's great values is the way that good things can be distributed. And many times your act of sharing may pay dividends in other ways— someone may share back!

4. Try General Reference Sources

Much of what is mentioned here about general reference is also valu-able for all the other subject areas as well. You can boost your research along by thinking clearly about what information you need. Knowing how to use general resources can often point you to more in-depth sources, just as looking at an encyclopedia article in the reference area of a library can help direct you to other works.

Online resources have been a particular boon to certain kinds of reference work. Online dictionaries permit you to look up words and even technical terms quickly, without owning the books yourself. Encyclopedias can provide useful basic information about various topics. Additionally, background information is provided by various other ready reference sources, which can include almanacs, and works such as the CIA World Factbook (http://www.odci.gov/cia/publications/factbook/index.html), which lists lots of vital data about other countries. One of the nice features of online resources on the Web is that they can often point you to other resources to further your understanding. For example, after looking up the linguist "Noam Chomsky" in the Britannica Online, and reading the information listed there about him, you can follow a link to his own home page, which allows you to read some of his more recently published work and find out more about his current activities.

Web search engines such as AltaVista, Google, and Northern Light are invaluable for locating resource material. And indexes such as Yahoo! are excellent because they divide information sources into subject areas, which makes searching for sources an easier prospect, particularly when you do not have a clear idea of where to start.

If you are running a lengthy project, keeping notes and a list of bookmarked sites (one of the features available from Web browsers that saves a list of URLs for future reference) will be a real asset. You can save yourself the sometimes time-consuming task of recreating a search, when you want to revisit a site you once examined, in search of more information or to verify something you did not note. Oftentimes it is worth downloading a particularly valuable Web page to save for later, if it holds addresses and other important information.

5. Explore Ready References:
Online Dictionaries and Encyclopedias

General reference covers a range of material, not always easily placed into categories. There are online dictionaries and encyclopedias, directories of people and organizations, lists of lists.

There is a handful of good online dictionaries presently available. Generally their Web sites include a search engine that allows you to type in the word you want to look up, and then your definition is returned to you. Yahoo!'s index lists several, including some specialized ones dealing with rhyming words and computer terms. One of the standards is the Merriam-Webster Dictionary (http://www.m-w.com/netdict.htm).

An intriguing site is the Reference Self at the University of California at San Diego at http://libraries.ucsd.edu/refshelf.html. This site includes a wide array of dictionaries, government resources, geographical lists and general online reference works. There are several other sites with a similar purpose (see, e.g., http://www.refdesk.com/).

A number of encyclopedias are available online, usually for a fee. At the moment there are only a few general encyclopedias available free of charge, one of which is *Encyclopædia Britannica* at http://www.britannic. com/). Several specialized encyclopedias exist, as well as some experimental attempts. Many of the "free" resources you find on the Internet are filled with advertising, which is one mechanism to subsidize what clearly is a lot of work. Other Internet encyclopedias enlist hordes of volunteers to assemble links to Internet resources. However, online encyclopedias have often become part of a university's reference holdings and have particular value for certain kinds of inquiries. These are often only available for the campus community.

Online use of an encyclopedia or dictionary is a different process than for its printed precursor, where you would page through a list of headings arranged in alphabetical order. Most online reference sources have a search mechanism, where the keyword of your topic is entered and you are taken directly to that entry. Some purists may miss the pleasure of idle browsing through the pages, where the distracting and engrossing adjacent entries often become more interesting than the original topic, but browsing is of course also possible in an online source, although accomplished by a different mechanism than paging through the volume.

"Ready reference" resources refer to an eclectic mix of information resources to which you may turn when looking for simple bits of information about a topic. This information might be the population of a city or country, conversion table for weights and measures, vital statistics on employment or religion, any of a wide range of data. This is one area where the Internet has provided an extraordinary opportunity for information dissemination.

6. Virtual Libraries

One notion of considerable impact currently under discussion and action is the Virtual Library, sometimes also called the Digital Library. This would be a "library without walls" where texts (and other documents) would exist in a "virtual" state, stored electronically and available to all who came visiting by an Internet connection. A number of universities and

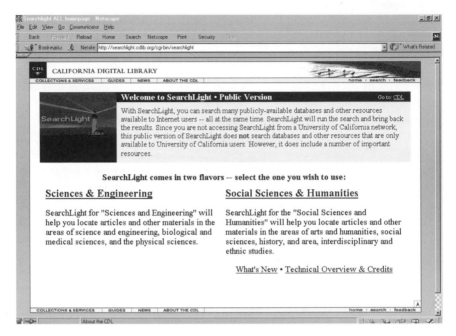

California Digital Library Searchlight *http://searchlight.cdlib.org/cgi-bin/search-light*. (©2000 The Regents of the University of California.)

other research institutions are now exploring the practicality of this sort of project, which in fact contains enormous implications in many of the arenas we have explored throughout this book, issues such as copyright, intellectual property, integrity of manuscripts, etc. Further, the time and labor required for copying manuscripts into a digital format is a daunting task. For a list of resources on Virtual Libraries, go to http://www.texshare. edu/TexShareServices/Professional/digital.html. Several other digital library endeavors are available also, in particular the California Digital Library Project at http://searchlight.cdlib.org/cgi-bin/searchlight/.

7. Find People or Organizations

On the Internet, just as in real estate, location is everything, and you are often in the position of wanting to communicate with someone without knowing her or his address. Luckily, there are some handy services that can help provide answers to the Internet address problem.

If you are not using the Web, and your potential correspondent has an address at a UNIX-based machine, from your shell account you can use the "finger" command to find her or his address. Thus if trying to reach me at San Francisco State University, you could use the following commands from your account "finger (name)@sfsu.edu" (substituting a last or first name in place of the brackets).

If on the Web, you can use one of a couple of finding services. These include WhoWhere at http://www.whowhere.com/, which is still one of the best, and Yahoo's own People Search at http://www.yahoo.com/search/people/, which also works for phone numbers and mail addresses.

Searching for people's addresses can sometimes be extremely problematic. Often the person's username (the first part of his or her Internet address) has little to do with the name. At the moment there are loose conventions attached to addresses, but they are hardly mandatory and thus not authoritative. Oftentimes a company will not make its list of users available to the searching mechanisms, perhaps fearing unwanted contact or an avenue for security breach of their computing resources. But these searching services are a vast improvement over the situation only a few years ago, when your choices were really only the finger command and having that person's address in hand (or on an email correspondence, business card, etc.).

Document Formats

Many online publications are increasingly available in PDF (Portable Document Format) style, meaning you need an Adobe reader to view them. A free version of this is available from Adobe at http://www.adobe.com/prodindex/acrobat/readstep.html. This standard is widely adopted throughout government publications, and is often used by online journals, since it preserves many of the traditional print-based features of a journal (the look and feel) while also making it more difficult to "cut and paste" the contents. The PDF format is a digital "photocopy," an image rather than a text file.

Humanities

The humanities constitute an area with a wide variation in types of resources. As a broad category, Humanities usually include the following disciplines: art, literature, philosophy, religion, and history. Each of these categories may have a bewildering range of subdisciplines. Art, for example, covers everything from the history of art, to architecture, music, performing arts, such as dance or theater, and fine arts, which can include ceramics, painting, sculpture, etc. Depending on your own interests, you may find some fascinating information at various Internet sites.

General Strategies

As with all research, if you are able to formulate your area of interest clearly, the first phase of looking for information is easier. If you have a relatively focused topic, doing a keyword search using a Web search engine may be an excellent starting point. An index like Yahoo! is also a valuable starting place, and there is a whole category titled "Humanities" in the Yahoo! index that divides into a wide variety of subheadings. The ability of the Web to deliver graphic files as well as plaintext is particularly useful for many humanities subjects, especially those with a visual component. Many art museums have made some of their collection viewable through the Web and can be a delightful source of study.

Yahoo! has a series of humanities indexes, and for long-term interests, you may want to try out one of the many mailing lists or newsgroups that discuss humanities issues, some of which are quite lively and erudite.

A Telnet connection to library catalogs gives you a chance to browse the collection(s), either by conducting a subject search or by using a keyword title search to find material. It is important to realize that libraries often have rare or valuable books, particularly of artwork, that might not circulate. They often reside in the library's rare book area or special collections. For some studies however, locating a rare resource may be a real stroke of luck.

When using a library catalog, a few subject peculiarities should be noted. Generally, the works of an author or artist can be found by conducting an author search, that is, by using the person's name in the author field. When looking for works of analysis (criticism, interpretation), one generally uses as a search term the person's name in the *subject* field. Thus an author search for Picasso will reveal a list of the library's holdings of his works (sketchbooks, collections of paintings, etc.), whereas a subject search will list the critical works, sometimes including exhibitions, about his creative efforts. Depending on what you are looking for, it is usually valuable to conduct searches in both author and subject fields.

Art

Internet resources for art are many and varied. For individual artists' works, and for other focused topics, a search engine is probably the best place to start. For more amorphous searches, an index is preferred. Coverage of various artworks is extremely erratic, and depending on museum collections (or sometimes even just someone's own personal obsession), there may be extensive examples available for viewing. As might be expected, coverage is sometimes improved when items have no copyright issues (i.e., when they are in the public domain, especially older works), although it is hard to see why a digitized version of a well-known painting (with a resolution of only 72 dpi) poses any real competition to a high-quality reproduction or the original.

One of the advantages of the Internet, and the ease of Web publication, is that minor or unknown artists are able to post samples of their work at their Web page, thereby achieving recognition that could be difficult to achieve by conventional means.

Some subcategories are better represented than others. For example, music, especially popular music, has extensive locations of material available. The old adage that "a picture is worth a thousand words" is absolutely the case online, with a slightly different meaning than the conventional one. Image files (as well as sound and movie files) are apt to be extremely large, often consuming much more than a thousand times the disk space required by the description in text.

This can result in extended "loading time," particularly if you are using a dial-up rather than a networked connection. Even fast modem speeds (56 Kb/sec) are slow compared to network cabling, and images can take considerable time to appear in a GUI browser. Other drawbacks can include diminished quality in the resolution of the images, again due to transmission issues.

Many museums make part of their collection available on the Web, although the digitized images can be disappointing in the quality of their representation. Two stunning, essential sites are the Louvre in Paris (http://mistral.culture.fr/louvre/) and the New York Metropolitan Museum of Art (http://www.metmuseum.org/).

ADAM: the Art, Design, Architecture & Media Information Gateway at http://adam.ac.uk/index.html has a large collection of Internet sites in a well arranged format with a productive search mechanism.

The Artcyclopedia, http://Artcyclopedia.com is a well organized very basic site that is excellent for a beginning search, and includes the capacity to search for artists and browse digital image files on the Internet.

The Art History Research Center at http://art-history.concordia.ca/AHRC/ has a focus on historical art studies.

The Art in Context.site is arranged by genre, artist, and discipline at http://www.artincontext.org/.

The Art Source page is heavily loaded with architecture as well as more general art links at http://www.ilpi.com/artsource/welcome.html.

A good commercial site is maintained by World Wide Arts Resources at http://wwar.com/ with a very nice collection of links to art sites.

Literature

Finding literary information on the Internet can be a real adventure. Like art, much of your success depends on the focus of your interest. Contemporary authors may not have much of a presence on the Internet for two reasons: (1) copyright and intellectual property issues inhibit dissemination of current works, and (2) there can be a fair amount of resistance in the traditional literary world to electronic (computer-based) technology. That said, there is a burgeoning community of online publication taking place, with zines and other electronic journals that discuss a wide range of issues. Some major authors have large followings in the Internet community, whereas others are almost untouched. Disciplines such as linguistics and language studies are also usually represented in this broad subject area.

There is a growing concern about the preservation of various literary works, and efforts like Project Gutenberg at http://www.promo.net/pg/ serve to identify and preserve in electronic format a range of significant literature. Mostly such projects have concentrated on monumental works of culture free from copyright issues by virtue of their age, i.e., works that have entered the public domain. Works such as Herman Melville's *Moby Dick* and Dante's *Inferno* have been translated into electronic formats and can be downloaded by an FTP connection or viewed on the World Wide Web. In general, the older and more famous the work, the more likely a digital copy is likely to exist. Medieval manuscripts have been digitally converted, along with a wide range of religious tracts. One of the drawbacks of this arrangement is the difficulty of reading a long (and often dense) work on a computer screen. On the other hand, one of the virtues of electronic copies is the ease with which one may conduct word searches either using a UNIX command like "grep" or a browser keyword search function. For detailed study of a manuscript, this can be a real boon and result in an enormous time-saving over traditional methods.

For Internet information on a particular author, the standard strategy would include use of a Web search service plus a look at Yahoo!'s listing of authors. The use of a commercial giant like Amazon.com at http://www.amazon.com/ allows you to check author's in-print work, while Bibliofind at http://www.bibliofind.com/privatelabel/welcome.htm is good for out of print items. Specialist commercial sites like Frontlist at http://www.frontlist.com/ cater to specific audiences, in this case avant garde literature. For long-term study, a look at one of the listings of mailing lists may also be productive. Telnet (and increasingly Web) connections to library catalogs remain a useful way of locating print literature, with the same techniques noted with artists in the subsection immediately preceding this one. Use an author's name in the author field to find works that the author has produced, the author's name in the subject field to find works of criticism and interpretation. Various journal databases, such as CARL UnCover, may be used to locate journal articles relating to your author.

Here is a list of general and specialist sites for more Literary research: A comprehensive, wide-ranging site called, oddly enough, Voice of the Shuttle (a quote attributed to Socrates) is at http://vos.ucsb.edu/. Medieval and early Modern literature can be explored at the Luminarium at http://www.luminarium.org/lumina.htm. A good gateway site maintained by the University of Alberta is Lit links on the Web at http://www.ualberta.ca/~amactavi/litlinks.htm. Contemporary Philosophy, Critical Theory & Post-modern Thought is the theme of http://carbon.cudenver.edu/~mryder/itc_data/postmodern.html. The Internet Public Library has an Online Literary Criticism Collection at http://www.ipl.org/ref/litcrit/. A professor at Rutgers University has a site devoted to Literary Resources on the Web at http://andromeda.rutgers.edu/~jlynch/Lit/.

Philosophy and Religion

Philosophy as a broad category and topics in religion are well represented in Internet resources. Most indexes have a section devoted to philosophy, usually located in a humanities classification, which as a major university discipline often has a determined presence on academic Web pages. Religion is found under "Humanities" and sometimes a category such as "Society and Culture" (as at Yahoo!). A fair number of original texts are available electronically, and as with literature the older and more major works are usually the prime candidates for electronic storage.

For starting places Yahoo! is an excellent beginning, located under the broad category of "Humanities." The World Wide Web Virtual Library has a useful section of philosophy resources, as well as lists of electronic texts and electronic journals (for which there are but few) at http://www.bris.ac.uk/Depts/Philosophy/VL/. Mailing lists cover both discussions of individual philosophers (e.g., wittgenstein@think.net) as well as broader categories (e.g., ETHICS-L@uga.cc.uga.edu). The WWW Virtual Library for Religion is a basic starting place for study at http://sunfly.ub.uni-freiburg.de/religion/.

The Internet is probably best utilized for philosophy by maintaining lists of resources and creating forums for discussion. The kind of reflective study necessary for philosophy is often difficult to do on a computer screen. Religion sites can offer simple information, often with an historical perspective, and are capable of dealing with current controversies. Although inconsistent in quality, nonacademic sites offer excellent compilations of resources.

Increasingly large numbers of religious tracts are being made available (one example being the Gnosis Archives at http://www.webcom.com/~gnosis/ with a remarkable number of relatively rare transcribed manuscripts).

History

There are some fabulous history resources on the Internet. The University of Kansas has a nice archive of material at http://history.cc.ukans.edu/history/WWW_history_main.html with indexes maintained by era and subject category. The World History Archive at http://www.hartford-hwp.com/archives/index.html has a broad choice of world history links. Ancient History is served by Argos at http://argos.evansville.edu/. Medieval history is represented by The Labyrinth at http://www.georgetown.edu/labyrinth/labyrinth-home.html with some online texts and beautiful examples of medieval art and The Orb, or Online Reference Books (http://orb.rhodes.edu/). One site useful for educators in Medieval history is the Internet Medieval Sourcebook at www.fordham.edu/halsall/sbook.html.

American History is represented at the American Studies Web at http://www.georgetown.edu/crossroads/asw/.

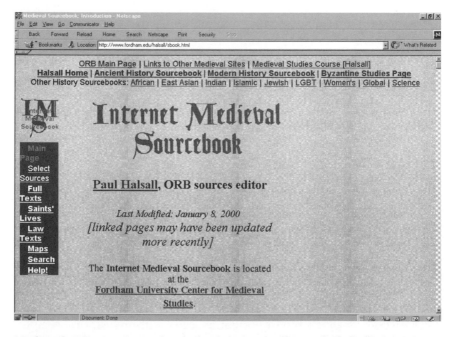

Medieval History Sourcebook *http://www.fordham.edu/halsall/sbook.html.* (Copyright Paul Halsall.)

The Library of Congress at http://lcweb.loc.gov/homepage/lchp.html and the National Digital Library at http://rs6.loc.gov/amhome.html have wonderful offerings, including images, movies, and sound

Social Sciences

Social Science Theory

The social sciences involve study of ourselves as humans—and how we communicate, think, act, conduct trade, procreate, produce tools, desire, and live. The social science disciplines range from the study of the human as individual (psychology, social work, and counseling) to studies of humans in broader contexts (anthropology, sociology, political science), and other subcategories defined by region, such as African studies and Middle Eastern studies, or other cultural group, such as Celtic studies and women's studies. Social science resources can include statistical data — births, deaths, income levels, ethnicity — from a census or other demographic survey. Gathering information can even include direct observation in a clinical or field setting. Often human subjects provide their own data in the form of diaries or surveys.

General strategies for research in social science areas depend a little on your own level of understanding and what kind of information you are looking for. The various divisions of social science are well represented among mailing lists, and for background material and specific questions, locating a promising mailing list is a valuable tool.

Various journal indexes can be extremely useful in identifying current, upper-level research on your topic. Telnet connections to library catalogs and journal databases such as CARL UnCover can often quickly provide lists of resources to pursue. The Web is an increasingly valuable location for social science information as more and more organizations make their resources publicly available. Other general strategies involve the use of a search service like AltaVista or Google or an index like the World Wide Web Virtual Library.

One good general site is Ohio State's gateway at http://www.osu.edu/units/sociology/indices.htm.

Psychology

Psychologists are interested in the ways humans, as individuals, think, learn, change, make sense of their universe, and act in a variety of situations. Social work and counseling in various forms may also fit under the categories of psychology and possess an applied component.

For background research on psychology in general, it is wise to consult a current text or other book, which can be located by perusal of your local library's catalog. The main library subject category is "Psychology," so you could use that as an initial search term. You will soon find that the subcategories branch quickly into a wide variety of topics, ranging from psycholinguistics to cognitive psychology. Yahoo! has a nice directory of the various branches with Internet resources at http://www.yahoo.com/Science/Psychology/Divisions/.

For more focused topics, good starting places are CARL UnCover's index to journal literature, which has good coverage of psychological literature. The main specialist database for psychological concerns is PSYCHInfo (in print known as *Psychological Abstracts*), which is put out by the American Psychological Association (APA) and may be available at a university or research library. You can also go to http://www.psychologie.uni-bonn.de/online-documents/lit_ww.htm for a good collection of online documents relating to Psychology.

A number of mailing lists and some newsgroups are devoted to specific psychological concerns, such as developmental psychology, clinical psychology, industrial psychology, etc. The Kovacs list, maintained by Diane Kovacs, is also available and searchable on the Web at http://www.n2h2.com/KOVACS/. This resource is an intelligent compilation of mailing lists for various subject areas.

Web resources include a fair amount of information on psychological organizations such as the APA, which have increasingly become ways to advertise conferences and other activities. A good list of organizations is at Wesleyan at http://www.wesleyan.edu/psyc/psyc260/psych.htm.

A marvelous gateway site, with extensive listings by format and topic is Psychology Resources at http://www.psychologyresources.net/site/resources.htm. A University of Washington graduate, Mike Madin, has a good site at http://academicinfo.net/psych.html.

Sociology

Unlike psychology, which is concerned with individuals, sociology deals with the ways that people conduct themselves in the framework of the society as a whole. Sociologists consider the qualities and defining aspects of large groups (women) as well as small (Jewish fathers). How these groups interrelate, communicate, and influence each other are the issues at the heart of sociology.

The Internet has been a highly attractive test bed for many contemporary sociologists, many of whom are intrigued by the way that the giant communications network has affected those who use it. The power and peculiarities of computer culture provoke a whole range of questions for sociologists: Do people communicate differently online than in face-to-face situations? What are the implications of an ability to present oneself in an ambiguous context such as the Internet? How are manners and social graces incorporated into computer culture? These sorts of issues are also apt to be classified in Internet indexes under the category "Computers and Internet."

Besides the general index, CARL UnCover, the standard database of journal citations for sociology is known as *Sociology Abstracts*, which in its online form is called Sociofile and may be available at a local university library.

Besides professional societies, the chief of which is the American Sociological Society, various Web sites are maintained by individuals and universities. Increasingly, leaders in a particular field are likely to have a presence on the Web, which sometimes can post important papers and links to other useful sites.

Ohio State maintains a useful gateway site at http://www.osu.edu/units/sociology/socres.htm. The University of Colorado at Boulder also has a good gateway with competent organization at http://socsci.colorado.edu/SOC/links.html.

Anthropology

Anthropology is a wide-ranging field that embraces a variety of inter-related disciplines. Cultural anthropologists study broad cultures, their evolution and differences. Physical anthropologists look at human skeletal remains in an attempt to discern the development of our species and its ancestors. Some anthropologists specialize in particular cultures or regions or even specific categories such as "aboriginal populations." To do this type of research it is often necessary to have multidisciplinary knowledge of anatomy, geology, and archaeology.

Various mailing lists are devoted to topics in anthropology, and the more important research areas have Web pages outlining current finds. The use of images on the Web is a great boon to those interested in anthropology because an image of an australopithecine skull, for example, is often highly evocative and worth many pages of text. The WWW Virtual Library for Anthropology at http://www.usc.edu/dept/v-lib/anthropology.html and Yahoo!'s "Anthropology" heading on social sciences are good starting places.

Area studies and other cultural group studies (Celtic, Jewish, women's studies) will likely fall under their own categories in an index like Yahoo!. Area studies are invariably interdisciplinary, and their component parts can be found either by searches under the area in question or within the umbrella of the broader category. If you were interested in agricultural practices in Egypt, for example, you might profit from both a look at Egypt-oriented sites, as well as sites connected with agricultural developments. The *CIA World Factbook* at http://www.odci.gov/cia/publications/factbook/index.html and various other government documents might give you some raw statistics, and you could incorporate a more advanced search with one of the search engines by combining the two concepts.

Political Science

Political science is the study of politics and political systems. It covers different forms of government and the ways that political powers are developed and utilized. The Internet, with its extraordinary communication potential, has had a particularly large impact on the discipline of political science because communication is such an important aspect of political culture. Many countries have great difficulty digesting the kind of uncontrolled (and uncensored) exchange of information that the Internet represents. Some political entities, such as the Democratic and Republican parties of the United States, have eagerly jumped on the Internet bandwagon as an avenue of extending party influence, but for other groups the Internet represents a threat to control. Since currency of information is so important to political scientists, the Internet becomes an attractive avenue for uncovering resources.

If you are looking for information connected with the United States, government documents may be invaluable. Besides voluminous statistics on all sorts of commerce, population, natural resources, etc., the U.S. government tracks international developments and provides data for a wide range of interests. The index heading in Yahoo! for government agencies is an excellent starting point: http://www.yahoo.com/Government/. Besides U.S. government resources, various international agencies and countries are listed. As mentioned above, many political parties have adopted the World Wide Web as a tool for their campaigns. During elections the major political parties develop lavish Web sites, complete with party platform information and contact information, to enable volunteers to assist the party's efforts. Political parties are likely to offer the text of important speeches on their Web sites, and they often articulate the party's position on a variety of issues. For U.S. politics, go to the Republican and Democratic party Web sites (http://www.rnc.org and http://www.democrats.org/).

A major tool of many contemporary political scientists is the online presence of many national and international newspapers. Often it is possible to browse a number of newspapers without actually physically subscribing to them in the traditional fashion. The *New York Times,* for example, is viewable at http://www.nytimes.com. Registration is required, as it is for many sites, and consists of agreeing to a standard contract by which you promise to use the service only for your own personal, noncommercial use and to abide by copyright policies. You pick a user identification name and a password, which allows you the privilege of browsing the newspaper and reading whatever articles are posted. Although using such a tool can have extraordinary value, one must resist the temptation to violate the copyright agreement by, for example, posting entire articles to newsgroups or otherwise interfering with the newspaper's need to maintain a solvent business. If the information is used for a report or written document, you of course need to cite the source carefully.

Here is a list of good Internet sites devoted to various aspects of Political Science: The Almanac of American Politics has lists of state elected officials and names, addresses and contact information for senators and other government officials at http://www.freedomchannel.com/almanac/almanac_of_amer_pol.cfm. The Political Reference Almanac at http://www.polisci.com/almanac/almanac.htm has a similar if broader (international) scope. The Yale Law School maintains a site devoted to historical political documents at http://www.polisci.com/almanac/almanac.htm. The University of Michigan has a comprehensive selection of political science resources at http://www.lib.umich.edu/libhome/Documents.center/polisci.html.

For International Political Science resources, see: The United Nations site at http://www.un.org. World Wide Web Virtual Library: UN Information Services at http://www.undcp.org/unlinks.html. Official WEB Locator for the United Nations System of Organizations (and Other International Organizations) http://www.unsystem.org. United Nations Scholars' Workstation at Yale University http://www.library.yale.edu/un/index.html.

Geographic and Environmental Studies

Research in the areas of Geography and Environmental Studies is often interdisciplinary, combining scientific research with social science inquiry. Some good sites for starting research include: University of Colorado Boulder maintains a Resources for Geographers site at http://www.Colorado.EDU/geography/virtdept/resources/contents.htm. EnviroLink Network at http://www.envirolink.org/. Global Environmental Information Locator Service (GELOS) is a European Union project at http://ceo.gelos.org/. The USGS Global Land Information System (GLIS) offers a wide range of geographic data at http://edcwww.cr.usgs.gov/webglis.

Education

Basic Education Resources

Internet resources on education are many and varied. Part of this wealth of information can be explained by the attitude of many Internet citizens—that the Internet offers fabulous possibilities for education at all levels and that exploiting its range, size, and speed is an entirely worthy endeavor.

Education resources break into several categories. One major resource, the ERIC database, is maintained by the U.S. federal government, but others are the work of dedicated people in the field of education who assemble their own lists of resources, curriculum plans, and educational materials. In particular, many mailing lists and newsgroups with an educational focus provide long-term forums for educational issues as well as short-term answers to the kinds of questions likely to arise in the field of education: What is a good way to introduce geography to second graders? How does English language acquisition proceed for students in bilingual households? What are the course offerings at the local community college? Finally, there is increasing interest in the varieties of ways that the Internet can further educational missions. Distance education is one such notion, with online classes and teaching that is done from locations remote from the "home" institution. But there are other ways to extend even "conventional" classroom activities that incorporate information technology and Internet protocols.

Identifying Your Interest

Before utilizing Internet resources, you will need to define your interests. Are you after specific information for certain questions? Are you interested in seeing what is available for a broad topic? Do you want to hook up with others with similar interests? Is your interest long-term? How much email can you deal with? Will you be contributing to a discussion or just "lurking"?

In general, if you have a long-term interest in a topic and wish to be connected to others with similar interests, mailing lists and newsgroups are valuable resource areas. If you are interested in higher-level research, the sort done by academics and scholars, then the ERIC index is an indispensable tool for identifying resources, which are increasingly available online, but you still may have to make visits to a university library to retrieve the journals as you would with CARL UnCover.

Many educators, particularly in the K-12 range, are open to online discussion and available for contact in a variety of forums. Many dedicated teachers have discovered the ease of self-publication on the Web and have constructed highly useful Web pages that include lesson plans, bibliographies, curriculum ideas, and a multitude of items. Finding them is not always an easy task; in fact, these kinds of home pages are resources that you are more likely to stumble upon rather than ferret out systematically, but they represent part of the wealth that the Internet has spawned.

Educational Institutions

For certain kinds of educational research, notably reviewing college and university campuses and their class and program offerings, the Internet has been a decided boon. These educational organizations, and increasingly other schools, have found the Web a wonderful way to widely distribute information about their philosophy of education, their campus and curriculum. Generally a campus home page is a good way to locate professionals in a particular field, with an opportunity to contact them for information. You can find these pages by using an index like Yahoo! to look under "Education" (http://www.yahoo.com/Education/tree.html), which has an expanded index, or by means of one of the search engines.

Although one should probably never base a decision regarding attending a secondary institution solely on that place's Web page, the Internet presence of a given college or university can contribute substantially to an understanding of it as an educational institution. Often you can discover the department course offerings, the current list of faculty members, and important facts about how the major is structured from the Web page. Recently it has even become possible to register online for various colleges and universities such as those in the California State University system. The advantage of such online information is obvious. The listings can reflect the latest changes and so are current in a way that a printed copy could never be, and the Web offers a wide distribution to potential students.

ERIC

One of the primary assets of Internet education resources is a government-sponsored office, called ERIC or the Education Resources and Information Clearinghouse, run by the U.S. Department of Education and the National Library of Education (http://www.aspensys.com/eric/). This is one of the few large, comprehensive databases around that is freely available to everyone. There are several parts to ERIC, but one of its greatest assets is the range of material it organizes. ERIC includes an index of a wide range of journal literature, conference papers, and research studies, all devoted to education, and is a must-see for nearly all education-related study.

The search engine employed by ERIC uses the principles outlined in our section on electronic searching. It is in a Web-based form, and you are given fields to enter your search terms using Boolean connectors to combine them. For general topics, you can enter search terms in the open boxes ERIC gives you for your keywords. You are also able to designate which field you want to search so that you could enter a person's name in the author field if you wanted to locate papers or articles that that person had written (rather than information about that person). For specific topics you could enter keywords in the "Descriptor" field if you want to search only in the list of standardized index terms. (ERIC also includes an online thesaurus of indexing terms, which you can examine to get ideas about subject topics.) It is a well-structured database, with a variety of searchable fields, and it delivers bibliographic information, or citations.

Although some full-text articles are available from ERIC (which is nice because you can read them right on your screen or save them to disk), many others must be located in one of several ways. Most universities, particularly ones with strong teaching credential programs or other education programs, will have ERIC documents, which can be identified in the database by their characteristic ERIC accession number beginning with the prefix "ED." These documents are usually archived as microfiche documents, although an alternative to this is to request a paper copy from ERIC itself for a fee. After your request, the paper will be mailed to you. Other materials indexed by ERIC will have an identifying accession number beginning with "EJ" rather than "ED," which means they are an ERIC journal. In this event you must make note of the journal name, issue information and date, and locate the journal in whatever library you have at hand.

One search tip noted earlier bears repeating here: Once you have found a "good document," one that reflects your topic of interest and is relevant, make sure to pay attention to the indexing terms (which ERIC calls "descriptors" and displays in the "DE" field) applied to that article and then conduct another search using those terms. This process of "chaining" by using alternative subject terms can often prove valuable for retrieving more relevant material.

Other Resources

One of the main assets of the Internet for education-related issues is the vast network of others in the field who are interested and have the time and energy to devote to an online dialog. Teachers and education professionals tend to be an extremely dedicated, dynamic, and committed lot, and much learning can take place by maximizing communication among the group.

Increasingly educational journals are available online, and one good source for locating such journals is a site maintained by the University of Wisconsin-Madison and Kansas State University at (http://www.soemadison. wisc.edu/IMC/journals/anno_AB.html). Many educators are interested in expanding the use of the Internet for educational purposes, and a flurry of activity centers on methods to deliver course content, bibliographies, discussion topics, and other aspects of learning through electronic means.

The World Wide Web Virtual Library (http://www.csu.edu.au/education/ library.html)is another useful starting point for Internet education resources. Often your specific educational topic is best approached through AltaVista or another search engine. Remember to use a variety of search terms, and that common words like "education" will occur in a great many documents so that such terms become useful only if used in combination with other search terms like "information technology" or "multimedia."

Correspondence courses have been a background footnote in education for decades, but the Internet has increased their impact considerably. As universities and other educational institutions have grappled with the difficulties of cost and reaching students that they might not serve otherwise, the notion of distance education has become ever more appealing. Technical difficulties abound, and the cost of transmitting real-time video of a class lecture, for example, over the Internet is daunting, but plenty of people are hard at work experimenting and improving methods of delivery for educational uses. For some subject matter, the online class works very well, and students' work can be submitted by email to a remote instructor, who can then respond with comments or feedback by email as well. Online "chat" conferences can provide a measure of interactivity to students. Despite many drawbacks to distance education, many educators will continue to use Internet technology to develop methods of learning.

Although education is one area indexed unusually well by one agency, ERIC, other subject areas that frequently overlap with educational interests include literature devoted to psychology, sociology, and some of the other social sciences. Language acquisition often falls into one of these categories, as does the subject of linguistics. The Carl UnCover database is another source for locating journal literature on educational topics.

Some other good Education related sites include: Center for Instructional Materials and Computing (University of Wisconsin-Madison) http://cimc.soemadison.wisc.edu/resources/anno_AB.html. Education Index Subject Guide http://www.educationindex.com/education_resources.html. Education World http://www.education-world.com/. HotList of K–12 Internet

School Sites arranged by state http://www.gsn.org/hotlist/index.html. Internet Public Library at http://www.ipl.org/ref/RR/static/edu0000.html. K–12 Curriculum Resources on the Web http://www.lloyd.com/k12curriculum. html. U.S. Department of Education and ERIC at http://www.thegateway.org/.

Science, Health, and Medicine

A range of science, medical, and health science material is available on the Internet, from databases of journal articles and drug information to lists of links to a wide variety of medical organizations and other scientific organizations. Increasingly, large amounts of scientific data are in digital format already, and for educational and other purposes it is not difficult to disseminate these data by means of the Internet.

Basic Resources

Yahoo! remains an excellent starting place for science, health, and medical issues, as does the WWW Virtual Library at http://vlib.org/Science.html. The categories for each are fairly clear and intuitive, and browsing them will give you an idea of what kinds of information is available. Newsgroups and discussion lists can be found at Kovacs at http://www.n2h2.com/KOVACS/ or Liszt at http://www.liszt.com/. The federal government provides an extensive collection of health and medical information through the home pages of the FDA (Food and Drug Administration). The CARL UnCover database at http://uncweb.carl.org/ provides a good journal index, particularly strong in science and medical journal listings. There are some online journals available, many of which require a registration process, often without any fee. One of the premier science journals, *Scientific American* is available online at http://www.sciam.com/.

As is typical with much of the rest of the Web, you may find that your searches lead to information involving organizations. A search on "diabetes" invariably includes a trip to the American Diabetes Association, which has an assortment of hypertext links to other sites with similar foci. When you have found a particularly valuable site, making a bookmark is probably an excellent idea.

Often university Web sites provide useful collections of links, which generally must meet the standards of university-level research and are consequently of value for any searching you may want to do. Some science museums, such as the Exploratorium in San Francisco (http://www.exploratorium. edu/), have intriguing interactive exhibits.

Some spectacular recent events, including stunning images from various space exploration forays, are listed at NASA's page at http://www. jpl.nasa.gov/. For physical science resources, particularly for instructors, see the Physical Sciences Resource Center, at http://www.psrc-online.org/. Physics has a large gateway at Tiptop at http://physicsweb.org/TIPTOP/ as well as the public section of the site of the American Institute of Physics at http://www.aip.org/public_info.html.

In the arena of biological science, Galaxy maintains an index of biology related sites at http://galaxy.einet.net/galaxy/Science/Biology.html and Harvard has a nicely organized set of links at http://mcb.harvard.edu/Bio Links.html. For a useful government maintained site, see the U.S. Fish and Wildlife Service at http://www.fws.gov/.

Here are some other specialized biology sites: For biochemistry see Biochemnet at http://schmidel.com/bionet.cfm. For botanical information, the USDA maintains a plants database of information at http://plants.usda. gov/plants/index.html. Zoological information is compiled by BIOSIS, the publisher for the *Zoological Record* and *Biological Abstracts* at http://www. york.biosis.org/zrdocs/zoolinfo/zoolinfo.htm.

Medical and Health Science

This is one arena in which the quality and reliability of the information offered is of supreme importance. Many sites, even those with impeccable credentials, offer disclaimers as to the accuracy and currency of the information they have compiled. A wise approach is to view Internet resources as a valuable tool for increasing your own understanding, but they should be utilized in a practical manner only in conjunction with standard, authoritative health and medical texts and appropriate advice from a doctor or other qualified medical representative. That said, you may find the Internet loaded with useful sites that include information on a huge array of medical and health issues. In particular, newsgroups and discussion lists provide an invaluable forum for discussion and community-forming interaction surrounding particular medical issues. For example, survivors of breast cancer have a discussion group that functions as an online support group to help provide information, support, and care to all who have been affected by breast cancer.

Most other databases are proprietary, and mostly unavailable to the public, unless your local library has arranged to subscribe to them. These include Medline, the standard index for medical issues, Index Medicus, and CINAHL (Cumulative Index for Nursing and Allied Health). For biotechnology issues, look at http://www.cato.com/biotech/.

Grateful Med is a version of Medline, the premier journal database for Medical Research and is freely available at http://igm.nlm.nih.gov/.

One of the standard medical reference works, the Merck Manual of Diagnosis and Therapy, is available at http://www.merck.com/pubs/mmanual/ with a "home version" (i.e. jargon free) at http://www.merck.com/pubs/mmanual_home/. A list of free medical electronic journals is maintained at http://www.nlm.nih.gov/.

There are several other valuable medical and health related sites. Achoo is a medical and health related site at http://www.achoo.com/main.asp. The Mayo Health Clinic has a site at http://www.mayohealth.org/ with a useful collection of news and journal articles among other items. The Virtual Medical Center at http://www-sci.lib.uci.edu/~martindale/Medical.html has a very extensive list of resources. For biotechnology issues, look at http://www.cato.com/biotech/.

When using one of the search engines (AltaVista, Lycos, WebCrawler,

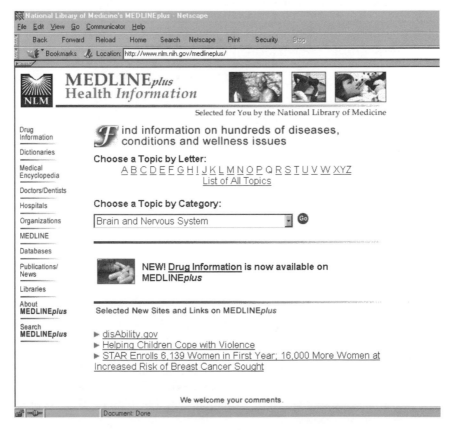

Grateful Med — Database of Medical Information. (Courtesy of the National Library of Medicine.)

etc.), remember that medical terminology is often extraordinarily precise. The medical community has a tightly organized controlled vocabulary, so that each symptom, disease, and drug is given an exact term. The main list of these terms is called Mesh, or Medical Subject Headings, and the proper use of these terms will greatly improve your searches. It is worthwhile to reflect that a popular term used in a search is more likely to retrieve information that employs the popular term, whereas a medical term from Mesh is more likely to retrieve information that possesses a professional perspective. When searching for topics such as AIDS, be prepared for an overwhelming number of documents. These highly salient topics generate not only documents from research organizations but also home pages of individuals coping with the syndrome and any documents that mention the term in any capacity. Often such broad topics are best searched either by using a hierarchical index or very precise search language with a search engine. (Instead of just "AIDS" use words that reflect your own particular interest, such as "AIDS and skin lesions" or "AIDS and pneumonia.")

Several government maintained sites (also listed in the government subject section) are excellent starting points for health related studies. These include: The U.S. Department of Health and Human Services has a nice site at http://www.healthfinder.gov/. The U.S. Government's Centers for Disease Control (CDC) at http://www.cdc.gov/ is an excellent site for authoritative statistics and information. The U.S. National Library of Medicine Site at http://www.nlm.nih.gov/.

Government and Legal

A multitude of U.S. government resources reside on the Internet, ranging from agency information and publications, to legislative, judicial, and assorted information that previous to the Internet's rapid growth usually were only found in government depository libraries. Those of you who have used government resources before will have respect for the complexity of organization required for this type of information. This is one area where it really pays to have a clear idea of what you are looking for. Is it tax information? legislative material? departmental information? In general, for government information, knowing the various departments and agencies and their responsibilities is an important precursor to successful searching.

The main divisions for government information break down by function. The judicial branch has information about the various levels of courts. The legislative branch lists directories for members of Congress, and provides avenues to examine current legislation and the issues connected with the Assembly and the Senate. The executive branch has information about the myriad federal agencies and about international concerns, such as foreign embassies and background data on other countries.

In general, the U.S. government has done a good job of making lots of information available. Besides providing basic information about their services, most government agencies and departments make their publications accessible, if not online then by providing forms or other mechanisms to order print versions of their publications.

Many publications are available only in PDF (Portable Document Format) style, meaning you need an Adobe reader to view them. A free version of this application is available from Adobe at http://www.adobe.com/prodindex/acrobat/readstep.html. This standard is widely adopted throughout government publications.

The Government Printing Office (GPO) makes an index available for government documents, many available online at http://www.access.gpo.gov/su_docs/tools.html. Some of the major databases available for searching include the *Federal Register,* the *Congressional Record,* and the *Federal Code of Regulations.* They have a search mechanism that can conduct searches in a variety of databases, which simplifies the process for the researcher.

Some related and highly useful sites include a site maintained by the University of California at Riverside called Infomine at http://infomine.ucr.edu/search/govpubsearch.phtml which has well-organized links to a variety of government sites. For contact information for senators and other government officials see the Almanac of American Politics at http://www.freedomchannel.com/almanac/almanac_of_amer_pol.cfm. For international issues, the United Nations page at http://www.unicc.org/ is an essential stop, with links to a great many countries and world organizations.

Legal Research

The legislative branch of the U.S. government is responsible for creating and passing laws for the benefit of the populace. One of the great benefits of the growth of the Internet is the increasing use of digital dissemination of legislative information. This is true at both the federal and state levels. Material that was once easily available only at "depository" libraries, which archived government resources for use by the public, is now available online. It is now fairly easy to track bills through the legislative process, view voting records of one's senators and representatives, and examine the debates that surface during the arduous process of creating new laws.

There are several places that list voting records, both for recent legislation and for past bills. Some of the sites that list this information are commercial, and their product is software that tracks legislative processes, whereas other sites are run by news networks or the *Congressional Record*. It always helps to know as much as possible about what you want (e.g., Senate bill number), but most of the searching mechanisms also work with keywords, so if you are not sure, you can use words or phrases (such as "gun control"). Available are standard government publications such as the *Congressional Record* (the official proceedings of Congress, including text of bills, voting records, etc.) and the *Federal Register*, which is a compilation of documents from the executive branch of the federal government. The Code of Federal Regulations is available at Thomas http://thomas.loc.gov/. The World Wide Web Virtual Law Library is also an excellent starting point at http://www.vlib.org/Law.html. The Cornell Law School has a nice site for U.S. Federal Code at http://www4.law.cornell.edu/uscode/. State statutes and legislative material is available in limited full text at http://www.prairienet.org/~scruffy/f.htm. United States Federal legislation is available at the U.S. Congress site at http://www.access.gpo.gov/congress/cong009.html. Another online legal resource is the 'Lectric Law Library at http://www.lect-law.com/. The level of complexity in government resources and legal research is fairly high, and readers are urged to consult any of the specialized works mentioned in the bibliography.

Business

Business research can take many avenues. You may be interested in a particular company's background and financial information. You may want to know how a particular industry is developing or about marketing trends in a particular region. Or perhaps you have a job interview with a company and want to be knowledgeable about its current situation and any events that may have bearing on your consideration for the position.

Of particular interest for business research is information presented by national newspapers, which can often be found on the Internet, although a subscription or registration process may be required. Many regional and national newspapers have an online presence, and sometimes you are able to search through their archives for older news stories.

It makes a great deal of sense to examine the source of your Internet resources carefully because there are great differences between the kind of information offered by journalistic sources, with a history of fairness and accuracy of information, and sources offered by marketing departments.

The ease and fluidity of electronic information only adds to the difficulties of evaluation.

Much business-related information has historically been strictly proprietary. Publishers such as Moody's or Standard and Poor's have made a name for themselves by a long tradition of yearly compilation of addresses, statistics, and business indicators for a huge range of companies and industries. They are not willing to distribute their hard-earned research for free and will continue to make their publications available only in a format that allows them to charge for their work. Other major business resources that are available online, such as LEXIS-NEXIS (a series of business, legal, and medical databases) and Westlaw (legal databases), continue to operate by means of paid subscriptions. There is nothing to suggest that these organizations will stop charging fees for their information, which is used in a very competitive environment, although the mechanisms for charging will likely evolve to better fit the electronic environment.

Company and Industry Information

The Internet has become a good source for information about particular companies and, to a lesser degree, given industries. Most companies maintain a Web site that provides background information and selected current news.

For many businesses, the Web has been a bonanza marketing device, but for every company that has done a good job providing information about itself, often in a form scarcely distinct from advertising, there are dozens whose efforts fall short.

For any particular company, the first stop for information really ought to be its own site, if it has one, and many do. The first step is locating the company's address, which can be fairly straightforward. You may have seen the address on advertising material somewhere (on television, radio, or a printed source). If you lack this direct information, you can try looking them up in an index like Hoover's at http://www.hoovers.com or Yahoo! under "Business/Companies" or conduct a search through one of the search engines. And sometimes it is worthwhile just to "guess" by applying a rough-and-ready Internet convention. The process of being assigned an Internet address is fraught with some high-stakes maneuvering, but most companies end up with their name somewhere in their address, and the general convention is to use a URL that begins with "www." and ends with ".com" and has the company's name in the middle. Thus Intel has http://www.intel.com/ and Coca-Cola is http://www.coke.com/. Sometimes you have to improvise, perhaps using an abbreviation or an acronym for a longer company name, but very often this trick works well.

Depending on the company's view of the 'Net and its approach to distributing information, it may offer quite a bit of material at its site. Among other things, it may tell you if the company is owned by another (has a "parent"). Remember, above all else, that a company's Web site is viewed as a marketing opportunity and that everything posted there is designed to reflect positively on that company, encouraging you to buy their products or services. This is not to suggest that companies do not offer other very useful Internet resources however, and more than a few companies make a lot of material available, either at their own site or by means of hyperlinks to other sites. But the general stance for you, the researcher, is to take whatever is offered you from a company's Web site with a considerable dose of salt.

There are other business-related places to examine, besides company home pages. These include information sites maintained by the various stock exchanges, government agencies, and international organizations. The pages for the stock exchanges not only offer lists of companies, along with their current prices and stock exchange symbols, but also offer links to the companies' pages themselves, a practice that serves as a very useful index.

When doing research on various companies, you should be aware of the differences between public- and private-owned companies. Private companies do not sell stock, whereas public companies are listed on one of the major stock exchanges and offer shares of their stock to the public for purchase. Public companies must disclose a fair amount of financial information — their stock prices, annual reports, and other financial information — as part of the public record. Private companies, on the other hand, are under no such obligation and can often be extremely economical about the information they make available. For such companies, often your best bet is to look for newspaper articles that may have been written about aspects of their activity.

One development that is occurring presently is the growth of what are called "intranets" or internal internets. Companies want to take advantage of some of the attributes of the Internet and apply them to their own organizations, to facilitate information sharing within the company or for special clients. This way various schedules, internal documents, or items such as software manuals can be easily made available within the company to any who may want to use them. Policies can be updated as often as necessary, and a great deal of simplification in the communication process can occur. Oftentimes these intranets go outside the boundaries of the company proper so that a software company, for example, might post upgrades, technical information, or even patches (software repairs) to their customers, who could only access the information by means of an account or password.

The University of Pennsylvania's famed Wharton school has a nice academic list at http://www.library.upenn.edu/resources/subject/business/subj-business.html. Forbes maintains a couple lists of interest, their International 800 http://www.forbes.com/tool/toolbox/int500/ and the US 500 http://www.forbes.com/tool/toolbox/forbes500s/. The Thomas Register of American Manufacture is an online directory which lists a huge number of American companies often including their catalogs at http://www.thomasregister.com/.

Traditionally one of the items of information necessary for much business research was the SIC (Standard Industrial Classification) code assigned to a given industry. This classification scheme has been superceded by the North American Industry Classification System or NAICS. Many resources still utilize the older SIC codes, however, in the way that they list their data and one of the standard reference guides, the Standard Industrial Classification Manual lists the classification codes at http://www.osha.gov/oshstats/sicser.html. For a comparison between these two systems, go to http://www.census.gov/epcd/www/naics.html which explains a little about the background of this change and provides conversion charts.

Marketing

Market research can take several avenues. If you are interested in starting your own business, you may be interested in a particular niche in your region. You may want to know about advertising or sales for a particular product. You might want to see how other businesses have used the Internet to promote their goods or services. You may even want to know about how much importing or exporting has been done for particular commodities.

Because the business arena is so competitive, a great deal of marketing information must be sifted carefully. Companies are not likely to divulge their successful marketing strategies in great detail if they think that their competitors could benefit from that knowledge. Generally, the end product of a company's marketing process is accessible, at its Web site or in some other format, and you can gain some sense of the company's overall approach by viewing and reacting to its efforts. Remember that a company's approach on the Internet, which despite considerable expansion still tends toward a demographic profile that is male, well-educated, and relatively young, may be very different from its approach elsewhere with a different audience.

For bigger overall trends, you may find it necessary to look through the marketing journals. Increasing numbers of online journals are devoted to marketing (see Yahoo! under "Business/Marketing"), but you may also want to use a journal index like CARL UnCover to find articles about your topic. Newspapers remain a good source for current marketing information as well, where you would use the search terms "marketing strategy" in your search terms. Consider also mailing lists and newsgroups, which can fill in gaps in your understanding.

Government documents have large amounts of data on importing and exporting statistics, so you may want to consult the GPO (Government Printing Office) index (http://www.acess.gpo.gov/su_docs) to see what kinds of data are there.

Some sites for international business information include: International Business Resources on the WWW http://ciber.bus.msu.edu/busres. htm. Bill Budge's International Marketing guide (with links) http://www. csus.edu/indiv/b/budgeb/intlmrk.htm. KU International Business Resource Connection http://www.ibrc.bschool.ukans.edu/default.htm.

Financial

Financial information can prove particularly elusive, and results may depend entirely on your interest. Certain data, such as current stock prices, are often easy enough to find by going to the source, in this case the stock exchange in question. Information like currency rates and national indicators like GNP (Gross National Product) are also generally available through government Web sites and International sites. But financial data on private companies can be extremely difficult to ferret out, and your best bet in that case is to look in newspaper sources in that company's region, in the hope that someone has done some reporting on that company.

Major newspapers such as the *New York Times* are available by free subscription, but many others call for a regular subscription to gain access to their online publications (one example is the *Wall Street Journal.*)

There are a number of subscription-only services as well, including Hoover's Online Business service and the Dow Jones. These often include extensive business information, including background information and financial data.

Other major financial collections include the home pages of the various stock exchanges such as the New York Stock Exchange at http://www. nyse.com/ and the EDGAR Security and Exchange Commission at http:// edgar-online.com/.

Popular Culture and Entertainment

For sheer entertainment value, the Internet is hard to beat. Although a huge amount of serious research takes place on computers connected to the Internet, a good deal of traffic devoted to pleasure and amusement also occurs, sometimes to the distress of those who feel they have more serious work at hand. With the Internet you can gossip, read postings from hundreds of others with similar leisure interests, play interactive games, and "talk" with others about sports, sex, movies, celebrities, and lifestyles.

Entertainment on the Internet occurs at many levels at many places. Newsgroups, particularly those in the "rec" and "alt" categories, deal with a bewildering array of entertainment topics, and it is instructive to consider the ten busiest newsgroups in terms of number of users.

The World Wide Web, with its graphics and ability to include formats such as video, audio, and other appealing formats, is (not surprisingly) the favored corner of the Internet for amusement. There are Web sites devoted to sports, television shows, hobbies such as car collecting, computer games, and wine making. Often the lines blur between entertainment and more serious activities, and newsgroups can serve both as valuable support groups for individuals clustered around a particular issue and as more casual social connecting points. Some Web sites permit a visitor to play a game of checkers with a computer, for example, or vote on matters of burning interest.

Cinema fans enjoy one of the Internet's favorites, the Internet Movie Database at http://www.imdb.com/. This takes advantage of the kind of function that databases do splendidly — making connections between various parts of their data sets. You can look up a movie, link to an actor's other works, check the director's output, and find connections all over the place.

If you have a specific interest, one of the search engines like AltaVista will generate a list of locations. Otherwise, probably one of the best starting points for any venture into the Internet for your own amusement is the Yahoo! index. Reflecting the extreme attention these topics carry, Yahoo! has three different categories for this aspect of Internet life, "Entertainment" (with movies, books, music), "Sports and Recreation" (including hobbies, cars, and games), and "Society and Culture" (people, sex, religion). The process of your own amusement is likely to be different from the kinds of research patterns advocated throughout this book, and it is very easy to spend hours moving from one page to another while soaking in the ambience unique to online life. You will discover that people have Web pages on the strangest themes and that the range of material available is enough to offend or attract nearly everyone.

Generally sites with content designed for those who have reached legal adulthood will have disclaimers and mechanisms to limit access. Sometimes this involves a registration process, and parents should be aware of various software applications that can screen sites with mature content from children.

New versions of amusement involving online communication occur in places known as MUDs (Multi-User Dimensions) or MOOs (MUDs of Object Orientation — graphic-rich MUDs). These are virtual areas, inhab ited by users who have logged in and who can communicate in "real-time" by typing at their keyboards. They are similar to "chat rooms" maintained by some commercial and other services, where online visitors may "enter" a room and converse with the other inhabitants of the room. MUDs differ in that they have a constructed environment that may be explored, as well as various "activities" or events that have been programmed into the environment. They are an outgrowth of the popular "Dungeons and Dragons" game now only played on the Internet, where players assumed various roles and participated in the game's progression through a series of increasingly difficult environments. MUDs have become modern equivalents of various traditional kinds of communities—cafes, taverns, local meeting houses. The virtual nature of the communication permits some interesting developments, but the overriding feeling is the strong need for a sense of community and for building relationships among the participants of these virtual worlds.

Appendix A:
Writing the Research Paper

Writing a research paper for an assignment at a high school, college, university, or other organization is a mark of scholarship. The research paper has a long and honorable tradition and serves several functions. Different types and styles exist, and a research paper may inform or present an argument, but any good research paper documents the researcher's efforts in uncovering information about a topic and presents insights developed about that topic. It leads the reader on a journey and points out evidence found and resources used. It sifts information and draws conclusions and demonstrates convincingly why those conclusions are valid.

A good research paper also acts as a product of pride. When written well and produced carefully, a research paper reflects on the author. When a paper is careless and difficult to read, it also reflects poorly upon the author. It is generally not enough to be meticulous in the process of uncovering information nor enough to be brilliant in one's ability to perform complex analysis of a difficult topic. If the results of these endeavors are not clearly communicated to the rest of the world (or to a target audience) then their value is minimal. Good research usually results in a product, which very often can be a research paper, and that product should demonstrate in the fullest way possible the excellence of the research effort. In this session we will discuss some of the theoretical concerns of a research paper and use a concrete example to show how the practical details can be addressed.

Beginnings of Research

What makes for a good research paper? Good research is an essential foundation for the finished product, and there are many steps to solid research. Many of the initial steps of research are covered in our earlier sections. These involve identifying a topic, defining a question, creating a search strategy, finding and evaluating potentially useful resources, and retrieving those resources for examination. All of these are covered in our earlier section, and we will group them as an initial block of steps.

Depending on the circumstances of the assignment or project, there may not be much choice over topic — you may be given one and instructed to find out everything you can about it and to report your conclusions within a certain time frame. Other times, for a senior thesis or a term paper, you may have the option of writing on any topic that has a relation to the class or your major.

Often an outline is suggested as a method for organizing a research paper, and for many researchers this is a valuable way to structure an inquiry. It can serve as a reminder that there are discrete stages to the process and can be extremely valuable in the final stages of writing because it helps keep the flow of the paper on a linear and logical path. Outlines can become drawbacks, however, if they constrain the inquiry too greatly. They must allow room for freedom of thought, the kind of spontaneous recognition of patterns that often serve so well in making sense out of apparently random evidence. Most research does not follow a smooth path but loops back and forth, experiences dead ends, and draws false conclusions. There are plenty of opportunities to go astray, and persistence and endurance are always aspects of good research.

Sample Research Project

For our example, we will be using a term paper assigned for an American history class. The focus is on the nineteenth-century. A friend and I were impressed by the large number of old house-foundations we saw while walking on an unpaved country road in rural Massachusetts. A stop at the local historical society revealed a map of the region in 1820, showing that indeed there had been a number of dwellings along the road that no longer existed on contemporary maps. Our initial question became, "Why were these houses abandoned?"

We dug a little more through records in the town hall and discovered that there were more people living within the town boundaries in 1820 than even as late as 1950, when the population gradually began to climb again after World War II. It became obvious that we needed to find out more about general population variations in the nearby area and in New England as a whole, as well as to find out more about other local conditions. We began our search through various sources. Using the computer in our dorm room at the university, we used a dial-up connection to the university library catalog and located several books on American population shifts in the nineteenth-century, town formation, and climate and economic conditions. Our first search was a keyword search (not limited to just subject headings) for the terms "New England" and "population," but most of the records we found were from recent census results. After finding one useful work, we looked at the Library of Congress subject headings in its catalog record and found the categories "Rural-urban migration — New England — History," "New England — Rural Conditions," and "Rural Population — New England." All of these reflected our interest, and we were able to pursue further searches using these categories as search terms for a search in the catalog's subject field. We used the database *America: History and Life* for finding journal articles on population changes in New England during the time period. We used our library to retrieve whatever sources we could and employed the library's Interlibrary Loan to retrieve other promising resources. Finally, we located a mailing list devoted to early American history and signed on for the semester. A lot of the initial information we uncovered was not particularly useful, and the general works often did not address rural populations as extensively as they covered Boston and other large cities. Despite this, we carefully examined the useful resources and made use of the books and articles listed in their bibliographies and notes for ideas about other sources.

• *Analysis.* After the initial phase of topic definition and information gathering, the researcher then employs the most valuable of all resources — the human mind. The information, which can be in a variety of formats, must be examined, sifted, viewed, read, turned over and over again, and contemplated from every possible angle. Although the level of research obviously depends on the skills and training of the researcher, no research at any level is possible without this phase of analysis. Whether dealing with primary data — a botanical specimen, a list of marriage records, a painting, a work of literature — or with secondary sources — books, film documentaries, and articles about the topic — the researcher must take on the topic with some passion and reflection. What is unusual about this topic? What are the first impressions? What conclusions can be made? Are there alternative explanations for what is going on? How have others approached this topic, and why do opinions diverge? Is there another way to look at it?

Analytic methods differ from discipline to discipline, and you must employ whatever methods that have been part of your education. Textual analysis involves dealing with the words written in a document, whether a novel, an essay, or an autobiography. Statistical analysis is employed when dealing with quantifiable data. Whatever methods are employed, the analysis must "follow" the information. As a researcher you must convince your reader that your findings are based on whatever patterns you discovered while you examined your sources.

Invariably, research involves going over the topic many times. Often one question leads to another so that what first appeared a simple question turns out to be extremely complex. This process will drive careful researchers back into their information sources to dig up other resources to answer their new questions. Sometimes the information uncovered seems inadequate, and more data is required, perhaps from a different perspective. In our example, initial efforts did not seem to address our original questions about the local population conditions of New England, and we needed to rethink our searching to focus more on rural populations. After reading background studies, we needed to think of what sorts of local data we could discover that might make sense in light of the bigger perspective suggested in the books we used. We needed to keep an open mind to possible explanations.

A systematic approach usually pays dividends for good research. It makes great sense to keep a notebook or other record of initial questions, resources examined (perhaps annotated to suggest where they were valuable or found wanting), and further areas of study required. Oftentimes it helps to frame questions visually, by drawing diagrams of the essential question and other questions that spin off the first one. Are the questions all clustered together, or do they take the researcher in wild and divergent directions? How might it be possible to answer them? Often, a research topic must be modified as it goes along, as the researcher grapples with problems of size and time. If the project has only three weeks for completion, then the topic must be framed in such a way as to be examined within those time limits. Invariably the researcher has to set some priorities and decide what issue is most important and capable of analysis.

My friend and I drew a diagram of our efforts so far. Our initial question — "Why were the houses abandoned in this Massachusetts town in the early nineteenth century" — was in the center of our page and had a big circle around it. We clustered other related questions and issues around it. What were the local economic conditions? Was there any evidence of sickness or famine? Did people migrate to the cities? Were the winters particularly hard for several years? Did any wars or local disturbances disrupt the population?

Some of these questions were answered fairly easily, but others demanded more factual material. Yes, there was some migration of people to the cities but not enough to explain the situation in this town. We decided to check conditions in other towns, and we read up on population movement throughout America in this time period. Sometimes we found too little source material, and at other times there was so much that it was hard to make sense of it all.

A good research paper benefits from the greatest amount of documentation possible. Much analysis takes place internally, as the topic is mulled over and over, but any mechanism to record that process, with notes, diagrams, even talking to others, will make the final process of production better. We kept our notes in a notebook and recorded ideas, answers, and suggestions from others.

We ended up covering a lot of different ground. We read about industry in that area of Massachusetts and how water power was used to run early factories but was gradually replaced by steam and other engine power. Advantages of nearby rivers for power and transportation yielded to the ease of more convenient power sources and railroads later in the century. Population records in other towns suggested that in general most rural towns did diminish in size during this period. Several studies pointed to the rapid growth of towns in the new territories of Ohio and areas west of the Appalachian Mountains. A question we posed to the mailing list directed us to a book, a published series of letters from a family that had moved from Massachusetts to the Ohio River Valley in the 1840s, and although the university library did not have a copy, we got one through Interlibrary Loan. The letters contained a lot of extraneous information but gave some real insight into the differing conditions of the two places. Farming was much easier in the Ohio region than in the rocky soil of New England. Land was cheaper; there were fewer taxes. The letters urged the New Englanders to join them in the new region. My friend and I had the beginnings of some clear conclusions.

Presenting the Results

One place where all researchers eventually become stuck is the movement toward actual production of the paper. Analysis can be endless, and often there is resistance to putting the findings into concrete terms. When the deadline beckons or the need for writing becomes great enough, however, the production phase must commence. We could go on forever, finding more and more material for our study, but the semester is coming to a close, and we have other classes calling for our attention as well.

If you have kept careful notes all along, often they can form the initial basis of the research paper. One vital concept to remember is that this is the movement by which the researcher explains his or her findings to the reader. Your notes may make complete sense to you — you have lived with this topic for some time — but they require expanded explanation for someone less familiar with the topic. Even if the intended reader is someone more knowledgeable than you, as is often the case in educational assignments, the successful research paper serves to place the topic into a useful and intelligible perspective. After working with details it is often difficult to see the broader landscape, but invoking the big picture gives greater weight to the research results. In this case we picked a very narrow area of study, the drop in population in one community, but were able to broaden the inquiry into a larger framework, the shift of population in America in the 1800s.

Good research papers convey some of the passion and attention to details of the research process. Enthusiasm is highly contagious, and if a researcher can convey some of his or her personal interest towards the topic, then the reader can be swept along with the process as well. As the researcher, you become the leader, and you have invited your reader to follow along on the journey you have made. The more you can permit your reader to travel with you easily, the better. Readers can trip over several things however, and it makes sense to be aware of common sticking points.

Act as a gracious leader. Try not to plop your reader down immediately in the tangle of your accumulated evidence. In an introductory paragraph or two, set the stage for the inquiry by describing the initial topic and the question or questions that developed around it. Explain what you are going to do in your paper, outline the kinds of evidence you will exhibit, and briefly indicate your conclusions. A good introduction should whet the appetite of the reader, whose interest you wish to arouse for the unfolding of the inquiry.

Poor use of language is a frequent stumbling point for any written document. It may not be possible for you to instantly transform yourself into a superior writer, but you can strive to eliminate points of vagueness, logical inconsistency, or lack of clarity. Any good research effort should leave the researcher a more conscientious writer. Use the best language skills you have, and if necessary consult style guides, writing manuals, and utilize the feedback of other writers and readers. Another pair of eyes or ears can often improve one's efforts by suggesting alternative words or phrases or even changes to the organizational structure of the document.

Unclear writing is often a symptom of unclear thinking. It is not unusual for your research to have had rocky moments, either in the uncovering of information or in the analysis. Mentioning this in the paper is sometimes helpful if it can illuminate how you overcame the difficulties. Good research mentions the methods used and why they were selected. You want your reader to identify with your decisions and to understand why you proceeded the way you did. Your last wish is for your reader to ask, "Why didn't you think of this aspect?" or to say, "I don't understand how you got from your evidence to your conclusions."

Try to anticipate problems or arguments opposing your conclusions. If you can demonstrate why objections to your analysis do not hold up against the evidence, you strengthen your own case.

In academic research it is imperative to support your conclusions by mentioning the research work done by others. In the course of our study of the population of a Massachusetts town, we read a lot of work done by professional historians. Their findings, done in the course of their own research efforts, represent scholarship with a reputation, and using their work lent strength to our own conclusions. Cite authoritative work frequently throughout your paper, especially if the ideas of those authorities have prompted you in some manner. Citing format depends largely on the preference of the instructor or the person responsible for the project. Different disciplines have preferred styles of citation. Historians usually use the Turabian style, an offshoot of the Chicago style, so we used a Turabian manual to create the bibliography for our paper.

Your paper, besides having footnotes or endnotes, should include a bibliography, or list of works used in your study. These sources are usually arranged alphabetically by author's last name and include basic information. Minimal information would be author's name, title of the work, and publishing information, including place and date. An example of a work used for our study listed in our bibliography in the correct format looked like this:

Barron, Hal S. *Those Who Stayed Behind: Rural Society in Nineteenth-Century New England.* Cambridge: Cambridge University Press, 1984.

This citation gives the reader all that is necessary to locate the work and proves that as responsible researchers we know enough not to appropriate the ideas of others as our own and to cite the works used and that we were careful enough in the use of our resources to keep track of them. If readers were interested in continuing the inquiry, the list would assist them in furthering the effort. Online resources, perhaps information gathered from the mailing list or a Web site, must be handled the same way as any other information resource and cited appropriately.

The paper should impress the reader by the careful manner in which the information was handled and the thoughtful and logical analysis demonstrated. It need not be flamboyant or flashy, which may, in fact, diminish its appeal. When you think of another researcher, you think positively of a careful and diligent worker, one who does not make rash decisions but is honest with results and strives for excellence at every turn. Your own work will be respected to the degree it follows these admittedly high standards. Humor and irony are occasional assets, but they should not get in the way of the main movement of the paper. Academics are people notoriously difficult to please, and your work may not merit the praise you think it deserves, but you do not want to give a reader any reason to think disparagingly of your work. Such reasons could include careless presentation, lack of complete documentation of sources, or advancing unsupported conclusions.

If you can accomplish all this, you will have a research paper that starts with a posed question, passes through a range of information sources that are carefully noted and described during the journey, and ends with a set of conclusions logically derived from the sources. Your footnotes and bibliography suggest the range of your inquiry and serve as a guide for anyone else who wants to make the journey, and as your tribute to the careful work done by others before you. If your paper advances the understanding of your readers, you have achieved no small success with your research.

Appendix B:
Citation Format

In the documentation phase of your research, you will want to make sure that you specify your resources accurately and completely for your audience. Traditional research has established a set of conventions for referring to resources used in a paper or published product. These conventions follow various "styles" adopted by their particular subject areas (for example, psychologists use the APA style developed by the American Psychological Association) that specify the form that the presentation will assume. Regardless of what style you use, the main goal is to be consistent in the way you document your resources (i.e., cite all of them the same way) and to include all the details necessary to locate the information. To take a look at some different styles, you can go to:

> Humanities: http://h-net2.msu.edu/~africa/citation.html
> APA: http://www.apa.org/journals/webref.html
> Chicago: http://www.apsu.edu/%7Elesterj/CYBER5.HTM
> MLA: http://www.mla.org/style/sources.htm
> Columbia Guide to Online Style: http://www.columbia.edu/cu/cup/cgos/idx_basic.html

When citing a book, the convention is for one to list document information that includes the author's name, title of the book, publishing company and date, and whatever page(s) you referred to. Journal citations include the name of the author, title of the article, the journal name, the volume number, and date and page number. All of this aids the reader in locating the information and indicates that you are careful enough about your research to note your sources. Furthermore, this action prevents anyone from accusing you of plagiarism — appropriating ideas other than one's own and not crediting the original thinker.

Internet resources pose a few unusual issues for citation, and their format is likely to differ from traditional citation format. As in all other aspects of the Internet, the address is of paramount importance. Besides including such information as title and author of whatever source you document, you need to indicate where you found it, which in most cases on the Web means including the URL. One convention started by Lui and Wang is to use the usual document information (author, title, etc.) and then follow in brackets a designation that indicates the document's online status plus the specific data connected with the location of the material. A good idea is also to indicate the date you found the resource, to let the reader know when you did your research because electronic resources can change so quickly.

Perhaps you have found a page on the Web that you used in research for a term paper. Using the APA style, you could cite that page in this manner:

> Hammett, P. and Dinkins, J. (July 2000). *Citation Styles & Formats.* Retrieved September 15, 2000 from the World Wide Web: http://libweb.sonoma.edu/research/citation/citestyles.html.

You may find that some of the information you want to use has incomplete data connected to it; for example, you cannot discover the author of the document or even when it was written. When in doubt, list as much information as you can about the document, never neglecting to list the address. As the Internet develops, there will be more standardization of this kind of information so that the citation process should become easier and conventions more universal. If you are creating your own documents, make sure to sign and date your work; this makes it easier for others to refer to your work.

If you cannot find the name of the person who is responsible for the document you are citing in the document itself, you might try viewing the source code of the document (on Netscape use the menu under "View" for document source). Often the name of the person who wrote the document is buried in the source code (in "comments" that are annotations surrounded by angle brackets), such as

> <!—written by Ned Fielden August 30, 1996.>,

or at least the name of the person who turned the document into source code.

Here is a selected list of style manuals to consult for further reference:

> Achtert, Walter S. and Joseph Gibaldi. 1985. *The MLA Style Manual.* New York: Modern Language Association of America.

ASA Style Guide. 1996. American Sociological Association. Washington, DC: American Sociological Association.

The Chicago Manual of Style. 1993. Chicago: University of Chicago Press.

Huth, Edward J. 1987. *Medical Style & Format: An International Manual for Authors, Editors, and Publishers.* Philadelphia: ISI Press.

Li, X., & Crane, N. B. 1996. *Electronic Styles: A Handbook For Citing Electronic Information.* Medford, NJ: Information Today.

MHRA Style Book: Notes for Authors, Editors, and Writers of Theses. 1991. Modern Humanities Research Association. London: Modern Humanities Research Association.

The Microsoft Manual of Style for Technical Publications. 1995. Microsoft Corporation. Redmond, WA: Microsoft Press.

Parker, Barbara A. 1985. *Journal Instructions to Authors: A Compilation of Manuscript Guidelines from Education Periodicals.* Annapolis, MD: PSI.

Publication Manual of the American Psychological Association. 1994. Washington, DC: American Psychological Association.

Style Manual: NEA Style Manual for Writers and Editors. 1974. National Education Association of the United States. Washington, DC: National Education Association.

Trimmer, Joseph F. 1989. *A Guide to MLA Documentation: With Appendix on APA Style.* Boston: Houghton Mifflin.

Appendix C:
Authoring Web Pages

There are really only two steps to web page creation (or three, depending on how you handle the coding), and certainly this simplicity is an enormous part of the appeal of the Web. People with minimal computer experience, but who have an Internet Service Provider, can have a page up and running in half an hour. There are classes everywhere on the development of this burgeoning little skill, from community colleges to extended education classes at colleges and universities, as well as online tutorials on how it works. Typically ISPs will make it fairly simple to set up a homepage as well, and often have good documentation. For a nice collection of web authoring sites, see NSCA's Primer at http://www.ncsa.uiuc.edu/General/Internet/WWW/HTMLPrimerP1.html or Larry Schankman's nice site at http://www.mnsfld.edu/depts/lib/html.html.

To make a webpage, you must first have some content. What do you want to publish? Your resume, your award winning bibliography on Baltic Archaeology, or your essay on Internet plagiarism? If you created the document at hand by means of a computer in the first place, you often have the option of saving the file in different formats, and many word processing applications will allow you to save your document automatically as a Web page. If however, for whatever reason this is not the case, your document must be turned from text to a form readable by a browser, and this is done by applying HTML (or something equivalent) tags to the document to allow it to format properly when viewed with a browser like Netscape Navigator or Internet Explorer. Simple text-editors like Notepad for Windows and Teachtext for Macintosh are perfectly adequate for simple Web pages, although it takes a lot of work to make a complex page with them. Many prefer the use of special web authoring applications like Frontpage from Microsoft, some of Adobe's offerings, BBedit, or Dreamweaver from Macromedia.

Here are the production steps:

1. Create a document in HTML or convert it with an editor. The simplest way to do this is to take a text file and apply HTML coding. The minimum tags are:

```
<HTML>
<HEAD>
<TITLE>Your Page's Title</TITLE>
</HEAD>
<BODY>
Your text goes here.
</BODY>
</HTML>
```

Some other formatting tags are listed later in the appendix, or see HTML Quick Reference from the University of Kansas at http://www.cc.ukans.edu/~acs/docs/other/HTML_quick.shtml.

2. Put your document in a place that can be accessed by means of the Internet. Your ISP may have a particular means for doing this, and you may need to create a directory (often titled "public_html") to place your file. You can do this in one of several ways. Sometimes you can create the document right in that directory, and when you name and save the file, the filename is attached to the ISP's URL for your own home directory, and the page is open for viewing. Thus, at San Francisco State University, my home page is listed as http://userwww.sfsu.edu/~fielden/ .

If you cannot create the document right in the directory, you need to move it there. FTP utilities allow you to upload your file to your internet Public Html directory, or you can resort to using the cut and paste options in a simple text editor to select your document's contents (with coding tags) and copy it into a file at your public Html directory.

Some Basic HTML Tags

```
<HTML> ... </HTML>Identifies the document as a Web Document
<HEAD> ... </HEAD> The head of the document
<TITLE> ... </TITLE>Title of Document
<BODY> ... </BODY> Main text
< B> < /B > Bold
< P >  Delimits paragraphs
< BR > Line Break
< HR > Horizontal Rule (Line)
< CENTER > < /CENTER >Center Alignment
```

< UL > < /UL > Unordered List
< OL > < /OL > Ordered List
< A HRFF="URI">Name of Page to be linked < /A > Links
< IMG SRC="image file" >Images

For those engaged in online publication of their research, or anyone posting anything to the web, a few broad suggestions will make life easier for the rest of us, who may be hoping to find and read your precious work.

Include important material in the appropriate fields, if available. Minimum information would be:

Title: A short, descriptive, unambiguous title is always best.

Authorship: Your name(s). If you have nice credentials to go with your name that may make a difference to the document and how it is received by others, it makes sense to include them.

Date of creation: Also date of revision, if it is a document that is likely to change frequently.

For many search engines, the metatag "keywords" and "description" fields are a productive place to list terms that might be used by someone who would be interested in your document.

One other piece of advice for would-be web creators is to get in the habit of discarding outdated documents that have lost their currency or value. Many of us have had the experience of crafting a good search query and submitting it to our favorite locating tool only to get a result set that includes a lot of outdated or otherwise useless documents.

For further information, see:

Castro, Elizabeth. c2000. *HTML 4 For the World Wide Web*. Berkeley, Calif.: Peachpit Press.

Garcia, Mario R. c1997. *Redesigning Print for the Web*. Indianapolis, IN: Hayden Books.

Graham, Ian S. 1998. *HTML 4.0 Sourcebook*. New York: Wiley.

Head, Alison J. c1999. *Design Wise: A Guide for Evaluating the Interface Design of Information Resources*. Medford, N.J.: Cyberage Books.

Lynch, Patrick J. c1999. *Web Style Guide: Basic Design Principles for Creating Web Sites*. New Haven [Conn.]: Yale University Press.

Musciano, Chuck. c1998. *HTML, the Definitive Guide*. Sebastopol: O'Reilly.

Niederst, Jennifer. 1999. *Web Design in a Nutshell: A Desktop Quick Reference.* Sebastopol, CA: O'Reilly.

Nielsen, Jakob, c2000. *Designing Web Usability.* Indianapolis, Ind: New Riders.

Spool, Jared M. c1999. *Web Site Usability: A Designer's Guide.* San Francisco: Morgan Kaufmann Publishers.

Bibliography

Abbate, Janet. 1999. *Inventing the Internet.* Inside Technology. Cambridge, MA: MIT Press.

Ackermann, Ernest C., and Karen Hartman. 1999. *The Information Specialist's Guide to Searching and Researching on the Internet and the World Wide Web.* Chicago: Fitzroy Dearborn.

Adams, Sharon, and Mary Burns. 1999. *Connecting Student Learning & Technology.* [Austin, TX]. [Washington, DC]: Technology Assistance Program, Southwest Educational Development Laboratory. U.S. Dept. of Education, Office of Educational Research and Improvement, Educational Resources Information Center.

Aggarwal, Anil. 2000. *Web-Based Learning and Teaching Technologies: Opportunities and Challenges.* Hershey, PA: Idea Group.

Ahuja, Vijay. 1996. *Network and Internet Security.* Boston: AP Professional.

_____. 1997. *Secure Commerce on the Internet.* Boston: AP Professional.

Albarran, Alan B., and David H. Goff. 2000. *Understanding the Web: Social, Political, and Economic Dimensions of the Internet.* Ames: Iowa State University Press.

Albert, G. Peter. 1999. *Intellectual Property Law in Cyberspace.* Laff, Whitesel & Saret. Washington, DC: Bureau of National Affairs.

Alexander, Dey. 1996. *Philosophy in Cyberspace: A Guide to Philosophy-Related Resources on the Internet.* Bowling Green, OH: Philosophy Documentation Center.

Allen, Moira. 1999. *Writing.Com: Creative Internet Strategies to Advance Your Writing Career.* New York: Allworth Press.

Ameis, Jerry A. 2000. *Mathematics on the Internet: A Resource for K–12 Teachers.* Upper Saddle River, NJ: Merrill.

Arnold, Stephen E., Erik S. Arnold, Ulla De Stricker, and Richard D. Fiust. 1996. *Publishing on the Internet: A New Medium for a New Millennium.* Calne, Wiltshire, England: Infonortics.

Ashbrook, Tom. *The Leap: A Memoir of Love and Madness in the Internet Gold Rush.* Boston: Houghton Mifflin, 2000.

Atkins, Derek. 1996. *Internet Security Professional Reference.* Indianapolis, IN: New Riders.

Bachrach, Steven M. 1996. *The Internet: A Guide for Chemists.* Washington, DC: American Chemical Society.

Barrett, Daniel J. 1997. *Netresearch: Finding Information Online.* Sebastopol, CA: Songline Studios. O'Reilly & Associates.

Barrett, Neil. 1996. *The State of the Cybernation: Cultural, Political and Economic Implications of the Internet.* London: Kogan Page.

_____. 1997. *Digital Crime: Policing the Cybernation.* London: Kogan Page.

Basch, Shari. 1999. *The Best of Internet Activities from Teacher Created Materials: A Compilation of Internet Activities from TCM Books.* Westminster, CA: Teacher Created Materials.

Basedow, Jurgen, and Toshiyuki Kono. 2000. *Legal Aspects of Globalization: Conflict of Laws, Internet, Capital Markets and Insolvency in a Global Economy.* The Hague, Boston: Kluwer Law International.

Battle, Stafford L., and Rey O. Harris. 1996. *The African American Resource Guide to the Internet and Online Services.* New York: McGraw-Hill.

Baty, S. Paige. 1999. *E-Mail Trouble: Love and Addiction @ the Matrix.* Austin: University of Texas Press.

Baumgarten, Jon A. 1997. *Business & Legal Guide to Online-Internet Law.* Little Falls, NJ: Glasser LegalWorks.

Bayne, Kim M. 1997. *The Internet Marketing Plan.* New York: J. Wiley & Co.

Becker, Henry Jay. 1999. *Internet Use by Teachers: Conditions of Professional Use and Teacher-Directed Student Use.* Report; #1 4006664926. Irvine, Calif. [Washington, DC]: Center for Research on Information Technology and Organizations, the University of California, Irvine and the University of Minnesota. U.S. Dept. of Education, Office of Educational Research and Improvement, Educational Resources Information Center.

Benson, Allen C., and Linda M. Fodemski. 1996. *Connecting Kids and the Internet: A Handbook for Librarians, Teachers, and Parents.* New York: Neal Schuman.

Bergan, Helen. 1996. *Where the Information Is: A Guide to Electronic Research for Nonprofit Organizations.* Alexandria, VA: BioGuide Press.

Bernstein, Terry. 1996. *Internet Security for Business.* New York: Wiley.

Berry, Michael W., and Murray Browne. 1999. *Understanding Search Engines: Mathematical Modeling and Text Retrieval.* Philadelphia, PA: Society for Industrial and Applied Mathematics.

Berryhill, Gene. 2000. *Designing Web Site Images: A Practical Guide.* Albany, NY: Delmar.

Bigham, Vicki Smith, and George Bigham. 1998. *The Prentice Hall Directory of Online Education Resources.* Paramus, N.J: Prentice Hall.

Bjork, Patrick Bryce, and Richard Cummins. 1999. *Reading, Writing, & the World Wide Web.* New York: Peter Lang.

Blair, Kristine, and Pamela Takayoshi. 1999. *Feminist Cyberscapes: Mapping Gendered Academic Spaces.* New Directions in Computers & Composition Studies. Stamford, CT: Ablex.

Boni, William C., and Gerald L. Kovacich. 1999. *I-Way Robbery: Crime on the Internet.* Boston: Butterworth-Heinemann.

Bosma, Josephine. 1999. *Readme! Filtered by Nettime: ASCII Culture and the Revenge of Knowledge.* Brooklyn, NY: Autonomedia.

Botto, Francis. 1999. *Dictionary of Multimedia and Internet Applications: A Guide for Developers and Users.* Chichester, NY: Wiley.

Bradley, Phil. 1999. *Internet Power Searching: The Advanced Manual.* New York: Neal-Schuman.

Brady, Regina, Edward Forrest, and Richard Mizerski. 1997. *Cybermarketing: Your Interactive Marketing Consultant*. American Marketing Association. Chicago, IL, Lincolnwood, IL: American Marketing Association. NTC Business Books.

Branch, Robert Maribe, Dohun Kim, and Lynne Koenecke. 1999. *Evaluating Online Educational Materials for Use in Instruction*. ERIC Digest; EDO-IR-1999-07. [Syracuse, NY]: Clearinghouse on Information & Technology.

Braun, Joseph A., and C. Frederick Risinger. 1999. *Surfing Social Studies: The Internet Book*. NCSS Bulletin; 96. Washington, DC: National Council for the Social Studies.

Briggs-Erickson, Carol, and Toni Murphy. 1997. *Environmental Guide to the Internet*. Rockville, MD: Government Institutes.

Burke, Jon J. 1999. *Intronet: A Beginner's Guide to Searching the Internet*. Neal-Schuman Netguide Series. New York: Neal-Schuman.

Calcutt, Andrew. 1999. *White Noise: An A–Z of the Contradictions in Cyberculture*. New York: St. Martin's Press.

Calvert, Sandra L. 1999. *Children's Journeys Through the Information Age*. McGraw-Hill Series in Developmental Psychology. Boston: McGraw-Hill College.

Chen, Guo-Ming, and William J. Starosta. 2000. *Communication and Global Society*. New York: P. Lang.

Cheong, Fah-Chun. 1996. *Internet Agents: Spiders, Wanderers, Brokers, and 'Bots*. Indianapolis, IN: New Riders.

Clark, Carol Lea. 1996. *A Student's Guide to the Internet*. Upper Saddle River, NJ: Prentice Hall.

Clement, Gail P., and Roy Tennant. 1996. *Science and Technology on the Internet: An Instructional Guide*. Berkeley, CA: Library Solutions Press.

Cohen, Eric E. 1997. *Accountant's Guide to the Internet*. New York: Wiley.

Conner, Kiersten, and Ed Krol. 1999. *The Whole Internet: The Next Generation: A Completely New Edition of the First — and Best — User's Guide to the Internet*. Beijing. Cambridge, MA: O'Reilly.

Cooke, Alison. 1999. *A Guide to Finding Quality Information on the Internet: Selection and Evaluation Strategies*. London: Library Association.

Cooper, Gail, and Garry Cooper. 1999. *More Virtual Field Trips*. Englewood, CO: Libraries Unlimited.

Crane, Beverley E. 2000. *Teaching with the Internet: Strategies and Models for K–12 Curricula*. New York: Neal-Schuman.

Cristal, Lisa E., and Neal S. Greenfield. 1999. *Trademark Law & the Internet: Issues, Case Law, and Practice Tips*. New York: International Trademark Association.

Cunningham-Andersson, Una, and Staffan Andersson. 1999. *Teachers, Pupils and the Internet*. Cheltenham: S. Thornes.

Davis, James B. 2000. *The Annual Consumer's Guide to Health & Medicine on the Internet 2000*. Los Angeles, CA: Health Information Press.

Davis, Richard. 1999. *The Web of Politics: The Internet's Impact on the American Political System*. New York: Oxford University Press.

Doheny-Farina, Stephen. 1996. *The Wired Neighborhood*. New Haven: Yale University Press.

Doherty, Paul Architect. 1997. *Cyberplaces: The Internet Guide for Architects, Engineers & Contractors*. Kingston, MA: R. S. Means.

Dowell, Jennifer M. 1999. *Writer's Guide to Online Resources*. New York: WANT.

Dowling, Carolyn. 1999. *Writing and Learning with Computers*. Melbourne, Australia: ACER Press.

Ebenezer, Jazlin V., and Eddy Lau. 1999. *Science on the Internet: A Resource for K–12 Teachers*. Upper Saddle River, NJ: Merrill.

Edwards, Margaret J. A., and Margaret J. A. Edwards. 1997. *The Internet for Nurses and Allied Health Professionals*. New York: Springer.

Ensor, Pat. 2000. *The Cybrarian's Manual 2*. Chicago: American Library Association.

Evans, James H., and Fred Horch. 1996. *Law on the Net*. Berkeley: Nolo Press.

Everard, Jerry. 2000. *Virtual States: The Internet and the Boundaries of the Nation-State*. Technology and Global Political Economy. London, New York: Routledge.

Ferguson, Charles H. 1999. *High Stakes, No Prisoners: A Winner's Tale of Greed and Glory in the Internet Wars*. New York: Times Business.

Fletcher, Patricia Diamond, and John Carlo Bertot. 2000. *World Libraries on the Information Superhighway: Preparing for the Challenges of the New Millennium*. Hershey, USA: Idea Group Publishing.

French, Deanie. 1999. *Internet Based Learning: An Introduction and Framework for Higher Education and Business*. Sterling, VA: Stylus.

Gallo, Patricia Anne Choban, and Michael G. Curran. 1999. *The 21st Century: Meeting the Challenges to Business Education*. National Business Education Yearbook; No. 37. Reston, VA: National Business Education Association.

Geirland, John, and Eva Sonesh Kedar. 1999. *Digital Babylon: How the Geeks the Suits and the Ponytails Fought to Bring Hollywood to the Internet*. New York: Arcade Publishing.

Gilster, Paul. 1996. *Finding It on the Internet: The Internet Navigator's Guide to Search Tools and Techniques*. New York: Wiley.

––––––. 1997. *Digital Literacy*. New York: Wiley Computer.

Glossbrenner, Alfred, and Emily Glossbrenner. 1999. *Search Engines for the World Wide Web*. Visual Quickstart Guide. Berkeley, CA: Peachpit Press.

Gonyea, James C., and Wayne M. Gonyea. 1996. *Electronic Resumes: A Complete Guide to Putting Your Resume On-Line*. New York: McGraw-Hill.

Graham, Gordon. 1999. *The Internet: A Philosophical Inquiry*. London. New York: Routledge.

Gralla, Preston. 1999. *Online Kids: A Young Surfer's Guide to Cyberspace*. New York: J. Wiley.

Greenfield, David N. 1999. *Virtual Addiction: Help for Netheads, Cyberfreaks, and Those Who Love Them*. Oakland, CA: New Harbinger.

Groves, Dawn. 1996. *The Writer's Guide to the Internet*. Wilsonville, OR: Franklin, Beedle & Associates.

Gumbs, Bob. 1999. *Internet Directory to Black Web Sites*. New York: Cultural Expressions.

Hacker, Diana, and Barbara Fister. 1999. *Research and Documentation in the Electronic Age*. Boston, MA: Bedford/St. Martins.

Halvorson, T. R, and Reva Basch. 2000. *Law of the Super Searchers: the Online Secrets of Top Legal Researchers*. Medford, NJ: CyberAge Books.

Hancock, Lee. 1996. *Physicians' Guide to the Internet*. Philadelphia: Lippincott-Raven.

Harcourt, Wendy. 1999. *Women@Internet: Creating New Cultures in Cyberspace*. London. New York: Zed Books.

Harris, Cheryl. 1996. *An Internet Education: A Guide to Doing Research on the Internet.* Belmont: Integrated Media Group.

Hay, Lyn, and James Henri. 1999. *The Net Effect: School Library Media Centers and the Internet.* Lanham, MD: Scarecrow Press.

Heide, Ann, and Linda Stilborne. 1999. *The Teacher's Complete & Easy Guide to the Internet.* New York: Teachers College Press.

Henninger, Maureen. 1999. *Don't Just Surf: Effective Research Strategies for the Net.* Sydney: UNSW Press.

Herman, Andrew, and Thomas Swiss. 2000. *The World Wide Web and Contemporary Cultural Theory.* New York: Routledge.

Herman, Edward. 1999. *Locating United States Government Information: a Guide to Sources, Second Edition. Internet Supplement.* Buffalo, NY: W. S. Hein.

Herring, James E. 1999. *Exploiting the Internet as an Information Resource in Schools.* London: Library Association.

Hill, Brad. 1996. *The Virtual Musician: A Complete Guide to Online Resources and Services.* New York: Schirmer Books.

Hock, Randolph. 1999. *The Extreme Searcher's Guide to Web Search Engines: A Handbook for the Serious Searcher.* Medford, NJ: CyberAge Books.

Hoffman, David S. 1996. *The Web of Hate: Extremists Exploit the Internet.* B'nai B'rith. Anti-defamation League. New York, NY: Anti-Defamation League.

Hutchinson, David RN. 1997. *A Pocket Guide to the Medical Internet.* Sacramento: New Wind Publishing

James, Henry, and David Freshwater. 1996. *The Farmer's Guide to the Internet.* Farm Journal. Lexington, KY: TVA Rural Studies.

Jones, Steve. 1999. *Doing Internet Research: Critical Issues and Methods for Examining the Net.* Thousand Oaks, CA: Sage.

Jordan, Tim. 1999. *Cyberpower: The Culture and Politics of Cyberspace and the Internet.* London. New York: Routledge.

Joseph, Linda C. 1999. *Net Curriculum: An Educator's Guide to Using the Internet.* Medford, NJ: CyberAge Books.

Kahin, Brian, and Charles R. Nesson. 1997. *Borders in Cyberspace: Information Policy and the Global Information Infrastructure.* Cambridge, MA: MIT Press.

Kardas, Edward P. 1999. *Psychology Resources on the World Wide Web.* Pacific Grove, CA: Brooks/Cole Publishing.

Katz, Michael, and Dorothy Thornton. 1997. *Environmental Management Tools on the Internet: Accessing the World of Environmental Information.* Delray Beach, FL: St. Lucie Press.

Keating, Anne B., and Joseph Hargitai. 1999. *The Wired Professor: A Guide to Incorporating the World Wide Web in College Instruction.* New York: New York University Press.

Kehoe, Brendan P. 1996. *Zen and the Art of the Internet: A Beginner's Guide.* Upper Saddle River, NJ: Prentice Hall PTR.

Kennedy, Angus J. 1999. *The Internet: the Rough Guide.* The Rough Guides. London. New York: Rough Guides. Distributed by the Penguin Group.

Kiley, Robert. 1999. *Medical Information on the Internet: A Guide for Health Professionals.* Edinburgh. New York: Churchill Livingstone.

Kleeman, Michael. 1999. *The Internet and Global Telecommunications: Exploring the Boundaries of International Coordination: A Report of the Fourth Annual Aspen*

Institute Roundtable on International Telecommunications. Washington, DC: Aspen Institute, Communications and Society Program.

Kolko, Beth E., Lisa Nakamura, and Gilbert B. Rodman. 2000. *Race in Cyberspace*. New York: Routledge.

Kollock, Peter, and Marc A. Smith. 1999. *Communities in Cyberspace*. London. New York: Routledge.

Kovacs, Diane K., and Ann L. Carlson. 2000. *How to Find Medical Information on the Internet: A Print and Online Tutorial for the Healthcare Professional and Consumer*. Internet Workshop Series; No. 10. Berkeley, CA: Library Solutions Press.

Kurz, Raymond A. 1996. *Internet and the Law: Legal Fundamentals for the Internet User*. Rockville, MD: Government Institutes.

Kutais, B. G. 1999. *Internet Policies and Issues*. Commack, NY: Nova Science Publishers.

Lai, Kwok-Wing. 1999. *Net-Working: Teaching, Learning & Professional Development with the Internet*. Dunedin, NZ: University of Otago Press.

Langford, Duncan. 2000. *Internet Ethics*. Houndmills, Basingstoke, Hampshire: Macmillan.

Lathrop, Ann, and Kathleen E. Foss. 2000. *Student Cheating and Plagiarism in the Internet Era: a Wake-Up Call*. Englewood, CO: Libraries Unlimited.

Lazarus, Wendy, and Kristin Lee. 2000. *Online Content for Low-Income and Underserved Americans: The Digital Divide's New Frontier: A Strategic Audit of Activities and Opportunities*. Children's Partnership. Santa Monica, CA: Children's Partnership.

Lee, Eric. 1997. *The Labour Movement and the Internet: The New Internationalism*. London. Chicago: Pluto Press.

Lee, Lewis C., and J. Scott Davidson. 1997. *Intellectual Property for the Internet*. New York: Wiley Law Publications.

Lehnert, Wendy G. 1999. *Light on the Internet: Essentials of the Internet and the World Wide Web*. Reading, MA: Addison Wesley Longman.

Lessard, Bill, and Steve Baldwin. 2000. *Netslaves: True Tales of Working the Web*. New York: McGraw-Hill.

Levin, Michael Graubart. 1996. *The Guide to the Jewish Internet*. San Francisco. Emeryville, CA: No Starch Press.

Libutti, Patricia O'Brien. 1999. *Librarians as Learners, Librarians as Teachers: The Diffusion of Internet Expertise in the Academic Library*. Chicago: Association of College and Research Libraries.

Lipschultz, Jeremy Harris. 2000. *Free Expression in the Age of the Internet: Social and Legal Boundaries*. Boulder, CO: Westview Press.

Loader, Brian D. 1997. *The Governance of Cyberspace: Politics, Technology and Global Restructuring*. London. New York: Routledge.

Maloy, Timothy K. 1999. *The Internet Research Guide*. New York: Allworth Press.

Mambretti, Joel, and Andrew Schmidt. 1999. *Next-Generation Internet: Creating Advanced Networks and Services*. New York: Wiley.

Mathiesen, Michael. 1997. *Marketing on the Internet*. Gulf Breeze, FL: Maximum Press.

Matystik, Walter F., Louis Theodore, and Roberto Diaz. 1999. *State Environmental Agencies on the Internet*. Government Institutes Internet Series. Rockville, MD: Government Institutes.

Mautner, Christopher J., Tim McLain, Vince DiStefano, and David Kershaw. 1999. *Educator's Internet Companion*. El Segundo, CA: Classroom Connect.

Maxwell, Bruce. 1996. *How to Access the Federal Government on the Internet, 1997*. Washington, DC: Congressional Quarterly.

Mays, Antje. 1999. *Legal Research on the Internet: A Compendium of Websites to Access United States Federal, State, Local and International Laws*. Legal Research Guides; V. 33. Buffalo, NY: William S. Hein & Co.

Maze, Susan. 1997. *Authoritative Guide to Web Search Engines*. New York: Neal-Schuman.

McKenzie, Bruce C. 1996. *Medicine and the Internet: Introducing Online Resources and Terminology*. Oxford. New York: Oxford University Press.

McKnight, Lee W., and Joseph P. Bailey. 1997. *Internet Economics*. Cambridge, MA: MIT Press.

Miller, Elizabeth B. 1999. *The Internet Resource Directory for K–12 Teachers and Librarians*. Englewood, CO: Libraries Unlimited.

Moran, Karen A. 1999. *Literature Online: Reading & Internet Activities for Libraries & Schools*. Fort Atkinson, WI: Alleyside Press.

Morgan, Nancy A. 1999. *An Introduction to Internet Resources for K–12 Educators. Part I, Information Resources, Update 1999*. ERIC Digest; EDO-IR-1999-05. [Syracuse, NY]: Clearinghouse on Information & Technology.

Morris, Evan. 1996. *The Book Lover's Guide to the Internet*. New York: Fawcett Columbine.

Morville, Peter, Louis Rosenfeld, Joseph Janes, and GraceAnne A. DeCandido. 1999. *The Internet Searcher's Handbook: Locating Information, People & Software*. New York: Neal-Schuman.

Moschovitis, Christos J. P. 1999. *History of the Internet: A Chronology, 1843 to the Present*. Santa Barbara, CA: ABC-CLIO.

Muller, Nathan J. 1999. *Desktop Encyclopedia of the Internet*. The Artech House Telecommunications Library. Boston: Artech House.

Munger, David. 2000. *Researching Online*. New York: Longman.

Naughton, John J. 2000. *A Brief History of the Future: From Radio Days to Internet Years in a Lifetime*. Woodstock, NY: Overlook Press.

Nesbary, Dale. 2000. *Survey Research and the World Wide Web*. Boston: Allyn and Bacon.

Nicoll, Leslie H., and Teena H. Ouellette. 1997. *Computers in Nursing: The Nurses' Guide to the Internet*. Philadelphia: Lippincott.

Notess, Greg R. 2000. *Government Information on the Internet*. Bernan Press. Lanham, MD: Bernan Press.

Novak, Gregor M. 1999. *Just-in-Time Teaching: Blending Active Learning with Web Technology*. Prentice Hall Series in Educational Innovation. Upper Saddle River, NJ: Prentice Hall.

Paul, Nora, Margot Williams, and Paula Hane. 1999. *Great Scouts!: Cyberguides for Subject Searching on the Web*. Medford, NJ: Information Today.

Peete, Gary R. 1999. *Business Government and Law on the Internet: A Hands-on Workshop*. Internet Workshop Series; No. 3. Berkeley, CA: Library Solutions Press.

Perritt, Henry H. 1996. *Internet Basics for Lawyers*. New York City: Practising Law Institute.

Plotnick, Eric. 1999. *Information Literacy*. ERIC Digest; EDO-IR-98-02. [Syracuse, NY]: Clearinghouse on Information & Technology.

Pollaud-Dulian, Frederic. 1999. *The Internet and Authors' Rights*. Perspectives on
    Intellectual Property Series; V. 5. London: Sweet & Maxwell.
Porter, David. 1997. *Internet Culture*. New York: Routledge.
Pottruck, David S., and Terry Pearce. 2000. *Clicks and Mortar: Passion-Driven
    Growth in an Internet-Driven World*. San Francisco: Jossey-Bass Publishers.
Provenzo, Eugene F. 1999. *The Internet and the World Wide Web for Preservice Teach-
    ers*. Boston: Allyn & Bacon.
Provenzo, Eugene F., and Doug Gotthoffer. 1999. *Allyn and Bacon Quick Guide to
    the Internet for Education*. Boston: Allyn and Bacon.
Randall, Neil. 1997. *The Soul of the Internet: Net Gods, Netizens and the Wiring of
    the World*. London. Boston: International Thomson Computer Press.
Reddick, Randy, and Elliot King. 1996. *The Online Student: Making the Grade on
    the Internet*. Fort Worth: Harcourt Brace College.
_____. 1997. *The Online Journalist: Using the Internet and Other Electronic Resources*.
    Fort Worth: Harcourt Brace College.
Reese, Jean. 1999. *Internet Books for Educators, Parents, and Students*. Englewood,
    CO: Libraries Unlimited.
Rodrigues, Dawn, and Raymond J. Rodrigues. 2000. *The Research Paper and the
    World Wide Web*. Upper Saddle River, NJ: Prentice Hall
Romm, Diane. 1996. *The Jewish Guide to the Internet*. Northvale, NJ: Jason Aron-
    son.
Rosenberg, Victor. 1985. "The scholar's workstation." *College and Research Libraries
    News no10 Nov 1985:546–9*.
Rosenoer, Jonathan. 1997. *Cyberlaw: The Law of the Internet*. New York: Springer.
Rutten, Peter, Ben Greenman, and Michael Wolff. 1999. *BotGuide: The Internet's
    Hottest Tools That Work the Web for You*. San Francisco: Harper SanFrancisco.
Schlein, Alan M. 1999. *Find It Online: The Complete Guide to Online Research*.
    Tempe, AZ: Facts on Demand Press.
Schwartz, James E., and Robert J. Beichner. 1999. *Essentials of Educational Tech-
    nology*. Essentials of Classroom Teaching Series. Boston: Allyn and Bacon.
Schweizer, Heidi. 1999. *Designing and Teaching an On-Line Course: Spinning Your
    Web Classroom*. Boston: Allyn & Bacon.
Seltzer, Richard, Eric J Ray, and Deborah S Ray. 1997. *AltaVista Search Revolution*.
    Berkeley: Osborne/McGraw-Hill.
Senjen, Rye, and Jane Guthrey. 1996. *The Internet for Women*. North Melbourne,
    Vic., Australia: Spinifex.
Shapiro, Andrew L. 1999. *The Control Revolution: How the Internet Is Putting Indi-
    viduals in Charge and Changing the World We Know*. New York: PublicAffairs.
Shields, Rob. 1996. *Cultures of Internet: Virtual Spaces, Real Histories, Living Bod-
    ies*. London. Thousand Oaks, CA: Sage.
Shiva, V. A. 1996. *Arts and the Internet: a Guide to the Revolution*. New York: All-
    worth Press.
Sikes, Alfred C., and Ellen Pearlman. 2000. *Fast Forward: America's Leading Experts
    Reveal How the Internet Is Changing Your Life*. New York: William Morrow.
Simpson, Carol Mann, and Sharron L. McElmeel. 2000. *Internet for Schools: A Prac-
    tical Guide*. Professional Growth Series. Worthington, Ohio: Linworth.
Slevin, James. 2000. *The Internet and Society*. Cambridge, UK, Malden, MA: Polity
    Press. Blackwell.
Smith, Darren L. 1999. *Web Site Source Book, 1999: A Guide to Major U.S. Businesses,*

Organizations, Agencies, Institutions, and Other Information Resources on the World Wide Web. Detroit, MI: Omnigraphics.

Smith, David E. 2000. *Knowledge, Groupware, and the Internet*. Resources for the Knowledge-Based Economy. Boston: Butterworth-Heinemann.

Smith, Roger P., and Margaret J. A. Edwards. 1997. *The Internet for Physicians*. New York: Springer.

Smith-Hemphiil, D. A. 1999. *CyberAssistant: How to Use the Internet to Get More Done in Less Time*. New York: American Management Association.

Soares, John, and Daniel J. Kurland. 2000. *Internet Guide for History*. Belmont, CA: Wadsworth.

Spector, Robert. 2000. *Amazon.Com: Get Big Fast*. New York: Harper Business.

Spinello, Richard A. 2000. *Cyberethics: Morality and Law in Cyperspace*. Boston: Jones and Bartlett.

Stacey, Nevzer. 1999. *Competence Without Credentials*. Jessup, MD: U.S. Dept. of Education, Office of Educational Research and Improvement.

Steele, Heidi. 1996. *How to Use the Internet*. Emeryville, CA: Ziff-Davis Press.

Stefik, Mark. 1999. *The Internet Edge: Social, Legal, and Technological Challenges for a Networked World*. Cambridge, MA: MIT Press.

Stein, S. D. Stuart D. 1999. *Learning, Teaching, and Researching on the Internet: a Practical Guide for Social Scientists*. Harlow, Essex, England. New York: Longman.

Stoll, Clifford. 1999. *High-Tech Heretic: Why Computers Don't Belong in the Classroom and Other Reflections by a Computer Contrarian*. New York: Doubleday.

Stout, Rick. 1996. *The World Wide Web Complete Reference*. Berkeley: Osborne McGraw-Hill.

Stout, Rick, and Morgan Davis. 1996. *The Internet Science, Research, and Technology Yellow Pages*. Berkeley, CA: Osborne McGraw-Hill.

Stuckey, Kent D. 1996. *Internet and Online Law*. New York: Law Journal Seminars-Press.

Stull, Andrew T., and James Puetz. 1997. *Political Science on the Internet: a Student's Guide*. Upper Saddle River, NJ: Prentice Hall.

_____. 1999. *Science on the Internet: A Student's Guide*. Upper Saddle River, NJ: Prentice Hall.

_____, Vitalius J. Benokraitis, and John P. Rossi. 1999. *History on the Internet, 1998–1999: A Prentice Hall Guide*. Upper Saddle River, NJ: Prentice Hall.

Swisher, Kara. 1999. *Aol.Com: How Steve Case Beat Bill Gates, Nailed the Netheads, and Made Millions in the War for the Web*. New York: Times Business.

Thomas, Brian J. 1997. *The Internet for Scientists and Engineers: Online Tools and Resources*. Bellingham, WA: SPIE Optical Engineering Press.

Travers, Ann. 1999. *Writing the Public in Cyberspace: Redefining Inclusion on the Net*. Garland Studies in American Popular History and Culture. New York: Garland.

Trinkle, Dennis A., and Scott A. Merriman. 2000. *The History Highway 2000: A Guide to Internet Resources*. Armonk, NY: M. E. Sharpe.

Turkle, Sherry. 1995. *Life on the Screen: Identity in the Age of the Internet*. New York: Simon & Schuster.

Valauskas, Edward, and Monica Ertel. 1996. *The Internet for Teachers and School Library Media Specialists: Today's Applications, Tomorrow's Prospects*. New York: Neal-Schuman.

Valovic, Thomas. 2000. *Digital Mythologies: the Hidden Complexities of the Internet*. New Brunswick, NJ: Rutgers University Press.

Vince, John, and Rae A. Earnshaw. 1999. *Digital Convergence: The Information Revolution*. London. New York: Springer.

Walch, James. 1999. *In the Net: An Internet Guide for Activists*. London. New York. New York: Zed Books.

Wall, Dave, and William Eager. 1996. *Using the World Wide Web*. Indianapolis, IN: Que.

Wallace, Jonathan D., and Mark Mangan. 1996. *Sex, Laws, and Cyberspace*. New York: M&T Books.

Wallace, Patricia M. 1999. *The Psychology of the Internet*. Cambridge, UK. New York: Cambridge University Press.

Wayner, Peter. 1996. *Digital Cash: Commerce on the Net*. Boston: AP Professional.

Wertheim, Margaret. 1999. *The Pearly Gates of Cyberspace: A History of Space from Dante to the Internet*. New York: W. W. Norton.

Williams, Bard. 1999. *The Internet for Teachers*. Foster City, CA: IDG Books Worldwide.

Williams, Joseph Ph.D. 1996. *BOTS and Other Internet Beasties*. Indianapolis, IN: Sams Net.

Wolff, Michael. 1999. *Burn Rate: How I Survived the Gold Rush Years on the Internet*. New York: Touchstone.

Wolinsky, Art. 1999. *The History of the Internet and the World Wide Web*. The Internet Library. Berkeley Heights, NJ: Enslow Publishers.

_____. 1999. *Locating and Evaluating Information on the Internet*. The Internet Library. Berkeley Heights, NJ: Enslow Publishers.

Young, Margaret Levine. 1999. *Internet: The Complete Reference*. Berkeley, CA: Osborne McGraw-Hill.

Zeff, Robbin Lee. 1996. *The Nonprofit Guide to the Internet*. New York: John Wiley & Sons.

Index